About the

Stephanie Brookes is a leading writer on modern spirituality. Her fresh, pragmatic and youthful approach appeals to a wide audience, leading to appearances on BBC Radio 2 and ITV's *This Morning*, and interviews in the *Daily Express*, *Company* magazine and many more. She is also the 'Destiny' writer for mybliss.co.uk.

How
to be a
Spiritual
Goddess

Bring a little cosmic
magic into your life

Stephanie
Brookes

piatkus

PIATKUS

First published in Great Britain in 2011 by Piatkus

A CIP catalogue record for this book is available from the British Library.

ISBN 978-0-7499-5301-0

Text designed and typeset by Sam Charrington Design

Printed and bound in Great Britain by Clays Ltd, St Ives plc

Piatkus
An imprint of
Little, Brown Book Group
100 Victoria Embankment
London EC4Y 0DY

An Hachette UK Company
www.hachette.co.uk
www.piatkus.co.uk

For John

Contents

	Introduction	ix
Chapter 1	What on Earth is Being Spiritual?	1
Chapter 2	We *All* Have Psychic Ability (Crystal Ball Not Required)	19
Chapter 3	Energy, Auras, Chakras… Oh My!	41
Chapter 4	Guardian Angels, Spirit Guides and Other Ethereal Observers	63
Chapter 5	Manifesting: More than Just a Flick of a Magic Wand	91
Chapter 6	Where, Oh Where, is My One True Love! Aka the Soul Mate	113
Chapter 7	Spiritually Cleanse Your Home	135
Chapter 8	The Goddess Hour	157
	One Last Thing…	185
	Acknowledgements	186
	Resources	187
	Index	189

Introduction

What comes to mind when you hear the word 'spiritual'? For every person who reads this question, a completely new set of images and ideas may spring to mind.

For me, when I first started getting into the more mystical side of life, I have to admit the images that came to mind were stereotypical to say the least. For one, the word 'spiritual' conjured up the idea of the quintessential hippie chick of the 1970s, with tie-dyed skirt, open-toe sandals and a tambourine in hand. Now, how many stereotypes did I just cram into that single image? Perhaps this is the image you have come up with too. Or maybe not.

For some people, the word 'spiritual' may sound a bit old-fashioned, perhaps the kind of word your grandparents might use. That, I believe, is the frustrating aspect of the word: it has far too many meanings and becomes totally confusing. No wonder the modern goddess cannot make head nor tail of what it really means.

I decided to take the word 'spiritual' and really consider what it meant for me. I knew from an early age that life was holding a special secret close to its chest. I occasionally caught sight of what was behind the 'ethereal' veil, but immediately retreated and pretended it didn't exist. Life's great hidden secret to me is what is commonly referred to as 'spiritual'. And it all boils down to this: life is bigger and more fascinating than we could ever imagine in our wildest dreams. Our personal potential is so vast that it would probably scare us to death if we ever fully grasped our true capabilities. And so 'spiritual', to me, is the understanding that life has a lot more to offer than first meets the eye.

My first experience of the spiritual occurred as a young child. It was only after a rather awkward confession in my late teens when I was informed that my spooky experience was not an encounter with a 'ghost' but in fact, with 'spirit'. To my astonishment, my confession was not greeted with surprise, or even mild concern for my mental well-being, but a willingness to help me to try to understand what I had experienced.

So why had I kept it a secret for so many years? What was I afraid of? Perhaps it was all tied up with the assumption that we were supposed to stop believing in such things after the age of 12.

In 2011, the idea of a spiritual realm no longer seems so far-fetched. These days we have entered an age of 'pick and mix': a time when we choose which aspect of spirituality fits neatly into our own personal agenda.

I believe today's modern goddess should be able to incorporate spirituality into her day-to-day life with the ease of putting together a brand new wardrobe. It should be varied, fun and a perfect fit that is uniquely right for her. This book offers an introduction to what modern spirituality can offer you in your life right now:

◆ How you can start to tap into your innate psychic ability.

◆ How you can utilise the angelic support that is around you right now.

◆ How to understand your soul, and how to spot that unique 'soul mate'.

◆ Simple meditative practices for you to learn, which can improve your happiness and well-being.

To the goddess who has chosen to pick up this book, whether you are a believer or you are undecided on the psychic or spiritual aspects to life, I say, continue to question. Spirituality is a subject like no other; it has no real beginning or end, and is an ongoing learning process that can only ever be defined by 'you'.

Spirituality has always been uniquely different from one person to the next. Buddhist monks, for example, often retreat to remote locations for years on end in order to meditate on the meaning of life. For the modern goddess, a meditation is often fitted in between a deadline and a shopping date with friends.

And that is exactly the way it should be . . .

Stephanie x

What on Earth is Being Spiritual?

*Y*ou've picked up this book, so the likelihood is that you are intrigued to find out what modern spirituality can offer you in your life right now. You may be thinking that you've coped thus far without this book, so how can it really be of benefit? The honest answer is this: you don't really have to incorporate or question any of the mystical aspects of life; in fact, you can probably cope quite nicely without doing so. But on the other hand, why would any modern goddess want to live half in shadow with only half the knowledge of life and its infinite possibilities?

You may be wondering where all this interest in the spiritual manifested to begin with. So, if you will allow me, I would like to take you on a mini journey into the history of modern spiritual thinking. I guarantee this will be the fastest history lesson you will have ever encountered.

A little bit about the history of modern spirituality

Spirituality is the practice and belief of philosophies concerning the spiritual – I know, it sounds like I'm giving a dictionary definition at this point.

These ideas and practices translated to the Western world not so very long ago, and came into prominence during the 1970s with a movement that was described as 'New Age'.

The New Age path of the 1970s offered a way for those individuals who had experimental feelings towards their spirituality and a need for a spiritual presence in their life, but who felt that religion didn't necessarily hold the answers. The movement ushered in a new wave of thinking about our very existence. It's fair to say that the movement was a lifestyle unto itself, but that doesn't mean it was a movement untouched by other influences. Part of what made it so unique was that the practices were directly from ancient religions and cultures from all over the world. Those influences stretch far and wide, from the East to the West.

One of the most important practices that crossed over was meditation (see Chapter 8), a practice that has permeated our culture, and something we are all aware of at some level. It is, perhaps, a practice that needs to be used more today because of the modern pressures we all face.

The defining image of the New Age brand has always been the peace-loving hippie, which is certainly not a negative stereotype but, as we all know, spirituality has moved on a bit from then.

On a personal note, I think you can be just as interested in the spiritual side of life in your stilettos and lip-gloss, as in sandals and a tie-dyed skirt.

The spiritual pick-and-mix

Your spiritual or mystical side (whichever term works for you is fine; or indeed choose a word that's a better fit for you) can be as little or as much a part of your life as you so choose. It's all about finding the part of your spiritual side that is uniquely right for you. You might, for example, want to understand more about guardian angels or how to see your aura. It's what I like to call the spiritual 'pick-and-mix'.

We pick and mix with every aspect of our lives, so why not our spirituality too? For example, we pick and mix with fashion all the time, every day in fact. We may team a fabulous vintage skirt with a high street jacket, and a bracelet you've worn since ... forever. It's what creates the vibrancy and variety of life. How dull would it be if we all chose our outfits, shoes and accessories from the same store? Not only would we look like a walking brand but it would also suggest a rather unadventurous attitude to life.

Spiritual Goddess tip

Modern goddess – The fabulous 'you': a woman who is not afraid to explore and question the spiritual aspect of her life.

Mixing it up is always the most fun. My secret pick-and-mix is a love of make-up and spirituality all blended into one. I bet you've never heard that sentence before. If I'm in a particularly 'girly' mood I find there is nothing more soothing for the soul than trying out a brand new look. I am always aware that colour (see Chapters 3 and 8) plays a major role in our lives, as it has a transformative effect on our entire well-being. It also has the power to bring out the different facets of our personality.

Incorporating spirituality is not about hanging wind chimes outside of every door or struggling into the lotus position for a meditation. It's simply mixing it up with your current likes or interests and seeing what happens. Whoever thought a lipstick or a jacket had the power to change how we feel about ourselves, but it can. Not only on an aesthetic level but a spiritual level too.

The Higher Self and the Lower Self

The spiritual and material aspects of who we are are often termed the Higher Self and the Lower Self. Our spiritual self is connected to our higher purpose, which we will be exploring throughout the book, and the Lower Self, or 'material', relates to the life we are living right at this very moment.

Understanding how our Higher Self and Lower Self work are the pivotal first steps to understanding our material and spiritual life. I like to call it the material–spiritual equation.

Our material life is the life you and I are living right at this very moment. As you read this book you may be curled up on your sofa with your favourite hot drink and a few chocolates, or you may be on the bus or train on the way to work or to see a friend. This is the material world in which we live, day in, day out, 365 days a year.

An average day in the material world might go something like this: wake up, shower, out the door, head to work or study, and then return home later that evening. Of course our day-to-day schedule changes, but we can all safely say we are familiar with the general framework of daily life, or the material life, you might say.

The spiritual life is the other half of life's great equation. This 'other part', often described as the 'mysterious and mystical presence' of our universe, is commonly viewed as a more alternative lifestyle, and not really a part of everyday mainstream culture. The material world, by comparison, is generally accepted as the way in which we live our lives, and yet the spiritual actually plays a much bigger role in our general well-being than we could ever imagine.

The spiritual is not as easy to define as the material; for example, our spiritual self is a complete mystery because we don't often see it. It isn't a tangible reality. We see a face staring back at us every morning when we look in the mirror, but we can't see what is behind or even around our exterior. It may even unnerve us to know that we each have a guardian angel by our side, but more on that later.

Also, the spiritual aspect to our lives has no boundaries, and the possibilities are vast. When you open your mind to the idea that you can live the life you truly want to live, you are tapping into your innate spirituality. Maybe you occasionally feel limited by the material world, and think that the life you have now is the way it will always be. By considering the idea that your life journey holds much more for you than just the daily schedule, you are already opening up to the idea of your true potential.

The trick with the material–spiritual equation is all about balance. Once you are near to 50:50 of both the material and the spiritual, life becomes richer and more fulfilling than you ever thought possible.

The 50:50 balance

Let me begin by introducing something we all share, a 'spiritual common ground', if you will. In today's world, finding a common ground with another individual can often prove to be difficult. Our lives are so crammed full with endless distractions and 'to-do' lists that we can often feel isolated from one another. Finding that special friend who shares and understands our interests, beliefs, and even worries, is a rare and special thing. It's comforting to know when someone 'gets' who we are. It's also a comfort to know that we are all similar on a spiritual level too, and that is where the spiritual common ground comes in. It is a part of daily life that we all face and, for the most part, we don't even know what it is we are dealing with.

The Lower Self

Let me begin with the Lower Self, which is the one we deal with at every single moment. It is that part of ourselves that makes us human. The Lower Self feels on a deep and emotional level. And it is that side of ourselves that builds attachments to material possessions. The phrase 'I want it *now!*' was most likely thought up by the Lower Self.

The Lower Self is an incredibly skilful operator, and is able to stunt you in ways that can go undetected for many years. Perhaps you put yourself down and feel that you don't deserve happiness. Maybe you have held off going for a better job because you feel unskilled, unworthy, incapable or fearful of the 'change' it will bring. You have probably noticed the quote marks around the word 'change'. Change is the last thing the

Lower Self wants to deal with. It quite simply doesn't like change, and will do everything in its power to stop it from happening.

It's easy to personify the Lower Self, because we all have, at some point, come into contact with another individual who is a demonstrable reminder of its debilitating effect. I think of the Lower Self as that so-called 'friend' we have all encountered at some point in our lives. You know the one I'm talking about: she always seems to make a catty slight about the way you look; it could be a passing comment about your hair that has all the subtlety of a sledgehammer; she loves nothing more than a good bitch about the rest of your friends, and you secretly wonder if she is doing the same to you; her insults are detrimental to your confidence, and you have probably wondered if it's fear that keeps you in the relationship rather than true friendship. This, ladies, is the best way to describe the Lower Self. The reason I compare the Lower Self to the negative friend is that the subtle but hurtful remarks keep you in a state of fear and that is exactly how the Lower Self likes to operate.

In more practical terms, it is that part of who we are that is fearful of change and of doing what we truly want to do. Have you ever received or been given a great opportunity, and then shied away? That would be the classic example of the Lower Self at work. The Lower Self wants you to remain in a stifled state of being, where you never expand or grow, or do anything that requires change.

We start to trap ourselves behind an invisible prison of uncertainty, where we gradually convince ourselves that 'we are not clever enough', 'not intelligent enough', 'not attractive enough' – until it actually becomes our truth.

Lower Self

The part of you that is fixed in the 'material'. The Lower Self can be unwilling to experience change, and is rather stubborn at times. The trick is to keep it in check and to make it work for you.

On a day-to-day basis, we also come across our Lower Self quite frequently on the weekend visit to the first floor of the women's department. Sound familiar? Your Lower Self loves it when you buy 'things'. The Lower Self knows those 15-minute fixes are temporary, and it's confident in the knowledge that there will be plenty more 'stuff' to feed its insatiable appetite. But as those discounts get bigger, so does our material world, and when we have filled our lives with enough material stuff, where do we turn to next?

Our material wants, needs and desires are perfectly natural and part of what makes us human. Perhaps the solution is nothing more complicated than striking that balance between the material and the spiritual. What could be better than spiritual fulfilment and 50 per cent off a new outfit so you can enjoy the best of both worlds! It all comes back to the 50:50 equation.

The Lower Self is the first step in understanding what makes us spiritual, as it importantly points out who we are in the material life. The Lower Self can, with training, be tamed and made to work to your own advantage. Your Lower Self is a part of your life, and a vital one too, so the trick is not to let it over-power you. A material and spiritual imbalance works both ways; for example, if your head is permanently in the clouds with all things mystical and spiritual, you may start to neglect all the great things in your material life. That would be seriously unbalanced, and not a practical way to live.

If we can understand how to keep the Lower Self in check, the more control we'll get back.

How to spot when your Lower Self is at work

- ◆ You doubt your own abilities.
- ◆ You think you are not good enough.
- ◆ You shy away from opportunities.
- ◆ You don't follow your own intuition.
- ◆ You follow what every one else does for fear of change.
- ◆ You don't stand up for yourself.
- ◆ You settle for second best.
- ◆ You're unwilling to speak up about what you want.

These are just a few examples to look out for when your Lower Self might be getting the better of you. Once you can spot the Lower Self at work you can start to change the situation.

How to control the Lower Self

The most effective way of keeping the Lower Self at bay is by acknowledging when you feel it has come out to play; for example, you may have experienced a rush of excitement from a new opportunity, and you just know it is something that you want to seize with both hands. It could be a great promotion at work, maybe you have been given more responsibility for a specific task, or perhaps you have been presented with the chance to go travelling with a friend; but then you start to feel yourself doubting and questioning your own ability. Once you have acknowledged that you have that fear or uncertainty, simply try to accept that is the way you feel. It isn't wrong or shameful to feel scared or doubtful; it is, after all, what makes us human. By accepting the way you feel, you won't have to deal with that same initial fear again and again. If you keep ignoring it, the same doubt will persist until you finally have to face it.

You can then decide what to do with the situation: let the fear take you over or deal with it head-on. Once you have come to the realisation that fear is nothing if you don't give your energy to it (and by 'energy' I mean valuable time which you spend thinking and fretting over that fear), you can release it and simply let it go.

On a personal note, I am something of a worrier, so the Lower Self has become my Everest in terms of learning how to conquer it. I know that all-encompassing feeling when your stomach is in knots and you simply can't get rid of your doubts and worries. So I have come up with the 'Face Your Fear Exercise', which can be a useful tool when a nagging doubt starts to take on a life of its own. If you feel there is something that you would like to do and know it would be a great opportunity or an enjoyable experience but you're rather apprehensive about starting out on it, try this exercise.

Exercise
Face your fear

1. To begin, sit in a quiet space where you won't be disturbed. Make sure you feel comfortable, as you will be focused for several minutes.

2. Start to visualise what is worrying you. (I like to shut my eyes for this exercise, as I always gain greater focus that way, but use whatever works best for you.)
3. Once you have a picture in your mind of what is bothering you, simply acknowledge your fear or the thing that is holding you back from doing what you want to do.
4. Be totally honest with what is bothering you, and don't be afraid to go into minute detail in your mind or even out loud. It is a good way of getting it off your chest.
5. Once you have that fear right in front of you, imagine holding it in the palm of your hand. Now, slowly bring your hands together and then crush that fear between your palms. Alternatively, you can imagine stamping it beneath your feet.

This simple but effective exercise helps you to take control of that fear and to simply let it go. You can adapt the exercise in any way you want; you may simply prefer to write all of your worries down on a piece of paper and then tear it up as a way of releasing them from your life.

Once you have let go of what is bothering you, it will then enable you to take on new challenges and to seize your opportunities. You are then in the perfect position to move on to the next level, which is the Higher Self.

An afterthought: do not worry if any nagging concerns come back into your mind, simply bat them away mentally with a firm 'NO'. You are the one in control.

The Higher Self

If the Lower Self can be described as the difficult friend, then the Higher Self can most definitely be described as your true friend for life. The Lower Self wants you desperately to remain in your comfort zone, while the Higher Self wants to get you going on your life's true path. The Higher Self is that truly great friend, the kind of friend who only ever has your best interests at heart. The Higher Self is in fact the real 'you', and can also be described as your spiritual self. The Higher Self knows your true talents and where you need to develop in order to flourish into the person you are meant to be. The Higher Self is that part of YOU who knows the great person you are, yet this part of ourselves is often the most neglected. Why is it that we always listen to our Lower Self when it is our Higher Self that holds the answers we are looking for?

The Higher Self wants you to work to the best of your ability and to progress, and it encourages you to develop yourself and to evolve as a person. The Higher Self can also nag at us (a bit like a well-meaning friend) and it is generally for our own good. My favourite example of this is what I like to call the 'lie-in scenario', which we have all encountered at some point in our lives. Have you ever woken up one weekday morning and felt that you just can't face the day ahead? You know that it's wrong, but the urge to pull a sickie is growing by the minute. What is it that stops you making that call to say you are ill? Is it guilt? Is it the fact that you are bad at fake coughing? Or is it that little voice inside, your Higher Self giving your Lower Self a little pep talk along the lines of: 'You're just being lazy, you've got to get up!' (Of course, on a freezing cold winter's day, the Lower Self might just win on this point.)

So now we know the Higher Self is most definitely on our side, but how do we know when that part of our self is communicating to us? Here are a few examples of when the Higher Self is doing its best work:

◆ You have a sudden feeling of intense joy and inspiration – it often feels quick and fleeting.

- ◆ You have a 'gut' feeling that something is right for you.
- ◆ You feel happy when you think about your study/career/ partner/friends, and so on – all sure signs that you are on the right track with these relationships and career choices.
- ◆ You feel inspired by life and want to achieve your goals.
- ◆ You simply feel happy and contented.
- ◆ You happily follow your instinct, as you know your intuition will lead you onto the right path.
- ◆ You trust yourself and your choices.
- ◆ You want your friends and family to be happy, and you gladly encourage and support them.

The Higher Self could be described as that elusive natural high. It suddenly hits you without warning, and when it does you feel invincible, as if you're capable of taking on the world. Your Higher Self also kicks in when you have received some great news or perhaps you have accomplished an objective or goal.

Higher Self

Your connection to your spiritual self. The part of you that wants to grow, explore, discover and fulfil your true potential.

It is often the case, when you feel most connected to your Higher Self, that your Lower Self suddenly decides to make an untimely appearance. Remember to galvanise your Higher Self when you feel your enthusiasm and confidence slipping. If you feel downcast, it can be helpful to repeat some positive affirmations.

A few confidence boosters

An affirmation is an upbeat and energising word or statement that helps boost your confidence and self-belief. Here are a few ideas to get you started (also see Chapter 5).

- ◆ I deserve happiness.
- ◆ I am a good person.
- ◆ I have lots to offer.

Vary the affirmations according to what suits you best. Every situation is different, and we all have varying degrees of how much we are influenced by our Lower Self, so always go with the affirmation that is uniquely right for you.

Another good tip to understanding when the Higher Self and Lower Self are trying to get a word in edgeways is that your Lower Self will argue and rationalise while your Higher Self will speak from the heart. With the Higher Self, there won't be any confused messages – it will be the pure and simple truth. Your Higher Self won't lie to you; it may be brutally honest at times, but it won't ever be false. Once you have mastered the two, you are already well on your way to becoming the ultimate 21st-century goddess.

Spiritual

An awareness of both the material and spiritual aspects to life: knowing there is more to life than first meets the eye.

The Spiritual Goddess first steps

Chat with friends A good chat with your closest friends can be a great way of opening up about new ideas on life. You might have an interest in angels, for example – an interest your friend hadn't realised you had. As soon as you start to open up new avenues of conversation you will find out so much more about your friends. On a personal note, I didn't open up to my friends about my spiritual encounter until the age of 19. I remember confiding in one of my closest friends and, to my surprise, she was thrilled that I had been so honest about my experience. She then went on to tell me how she had also felt a spiritual presence around her in her bedroom, and that it occurred quite regularly. It was a breakthrough moment in our friendship, and from then on we became more open about everything, from the latest reality TV addiction to the new spiritual developments in our lives.

The Higher Self and Lower Self talk By yourself or with a friend, start to make a list of what you think are the main examples of when your Lower Self is making its presence known. You may be having a great day, and suddenly feel a bit out of sorts, perhaps you have started to focus on the negative – and you know how your Lower Self likes nothing more than to keep you that way. Note it down as a prompt, so that you can swiftly bring in your Higher Self to sort out the situation.

To combat the Lower Self write down what it is that gives you that rush of excitement or energy, or what makes you feel good about yourself. Anything that lifts your spirits is a sure sign that your Higher Self is communicating to you and that you're on the right track.

Below is my personal Higher Self list to start you off: I feel my spirit soaring (quite literally!) when:

- I chat with a good friend.
- I am sitting in the park, reading a good book.
- I'm watching my favourite movie with a bowl of popcorn.

We all have our secret activities that make us feel good about ourselves. Your Higher Self list should contain all those personal pleasures that just put you in a better mood. Simple pleasures are always the best. If you feel the Lower Self taking over, simply replace it with a positive thought or, even better, a positive action from your list. As soon as we make those activities a bigger part of our lives, the more we allow ourselves to feel happier.

Visual prompts act as an effective way of reminding us what we truly love doing. It's sometimes easy to forget.

Mix it up I mentioned the pick-and-mix aspect of spirituality earlier, and for the modern goddess who has a lot going on in her life already, being selective about what you choose to do can be a great starting-off point for your burgeoning spiritual journey. For anyone who has just dipped their toes into the subject, this book offers a thorough introduction to a variety of spiritual practices, and we will look into everything from learning how to do an effective meditation, manifesting your dreams, and aura work, right through to learning about your Guardian Angel. The variety is quite significant, so there is something for everyone. You may even find that you want to know a bit about everything and then decide if there's something worth exploring more. It is all a choice, not a requirement. So enjoy finding out more, but don't overwhelm yourself. In finding out about any new subject, always go at your own pace and never feel rushed. Above all, it should be fun and relevant to *you*.

Ask questions We worry that if we ask a question, or admit to not knowing something, it somehow reflects badly on us. It was once the case that when a new subject interested me or I had a query, I was often afraid to ask for fear of sounding stupid; for example, I knew that I had seen what I thought was a ghost, but if I had asked or questioned more I would have found out that a 'ghost' wasn't exactly the whole truth. On TV, in magazines and in film we see and read much about ghosts, spirit guides, angels, and so on, but it doesn't often go into the nitty-gritty of what might really be going on. Asking questions and questioning in general is perhaps the most important of all the steps to under-standing not only the spiritual world around us but the world of spirit within us too, which is perhaps the most exciting aspect of all.

A spiritual start

A subject as vast as the spiritual is a daunting prospect. Where do you even start? That was the question I asked myself as I first launched into this chapter. It quickly dawned on me that sharing my personal experiences might also reflect the experiences of other young women. I think the very act of sharing is something women, in particular, can all relate to. We are all in the same boat emotionally: we share similar fears with our work, relation-ships and friendships and it makes perfect sense that we are all similar on a spiritual level too. After all, we are all operating in the material world; our lessons to learn and life choices may be different, but we're all striving to do the best we can with our lives. Spiritually speaking, that's what it's all about. And as you work through this book, I hope the ideas and practices bring you closer to all your fabulous possibilities.

We All Have Psychic Ability (Crystal Ball Not Required)

If you could look into your own crystal ball, what would you hope to see? Would you like your future to be clearly mapped out for you, or would you rather a journey of yet undiscovered possibilities?

Years ago, in my teenage haste, I attempted to uncover what my future had in store for me, and I visited a local fortune-teller. It was an experience I remember to this day, not least because the crystal ball was, in fact, an upside-down goldfish bowl. It was on the tip of my tongue to point out the unusual psychic tool of choice, yet I managed to stifle my observation and pretended I hadn't noticed.

I watched intently as the fortune-teller began to immerse in her psychic vision: eyes flashing wildly, hands swirling about the goldfish bowl in typically dramatic fashion, and the only real question on my mind, and I imagine every other paying customer that day, was: 'What happened to the fish?' Suffice to say, the information I received didn't really ring true for me.

Unsurprisingly, I was put off crystal balls for life. But seriously, when it comes to crystal balls – although a perfectly good psychic tool (when the crystal ball is in fact a crystal ball!) – I knew that crystal gazing wasn't my psychic preference. I wanted to find out if it was possible to learn more about the psychic world in a way that was easy for me and my friends to practise; a way that was simple and without too much fuss.

The idea that we all hold the ability to unlock our psychic potential was enough to whet my psychic appetite. I also knew that although I had encountered a spirit presence years before, I didn't know much about what the psychic world really involved. You may be wondering the same thing. We generally overlook our psychic self, because it isn't something that is openly discussed in everyday conversation, or embraced as a subject of mainstream study – I don't think I ever saw 'psychic development' on the school curriculum. It would have made a welcome addition after double maths, at least in my case anyway.

It's an exciting truth that we *all* possess some degree of psychic ability. This ability is often strongly felt in our younger years, before the conditioning to the adult world dispels any notion of such things. This ability then starts to decline during adolescence as we enter adulthood, yet that potential is not entirely extinguished, and it can be reignited at any time.

In the media arena today, we are experiencing something of a psychic renaissance. On TV, in magazines and in newspapers, people are openly discussing their own psychic encounters. It ultimately leads us to question whether we too have experienced any kind of phenomena in our own life.

In fact, we experience psychic happenings all the time, sometimes without even noticing. You may recognise yourself in the scenarios on the next page.

Your everyday psychic happenings

◆ You walk into a room and, for some reason unbeknown to you, it just doesn't feel right. The atmosphere feels negative, it may even make you feel sad, and within a matter of moments you know you need to leave.

◆ A distant friend or relative who you haven't heard from in a long time suddenly pops into your mind for no apparent reason. You then receive a telephone call from that person a few days later or you bump into them unexpectedly on the street.

These are examples of everyday psychic happenings. You may be wondering what makes them 'psychic' in the first place – all will be revealed later in the book, so stay tuned.

'You have the gift!' Correction: we *all* do

I often notice from the media perception of psychic ability, and also from discussion over the years, that any form of psychic ability is often seen as a 'gift', and only humbled upon a chosen few. I find this a frustrating perception, as everyone has the ability to develop this skill.

I want to mention this point here and now, because I wouldn't want you to think that if you haven't felt or experienced any kind of psychic experience before, you have missed the psychic boat, so to speak.

OK, let's be honest, we know there are some individuals out there who possess an incredible natural psychic ability, a skill they would have been born with. For the majority of us (me included) it takes a lot more time and effort.

With plenty of practice, however, we can all strengthen this innate skill. In fact, you may discover you have more ability in this area than you ever thought possible.

The psychic and the senses

We have five senses:

- ◆ Touch
- ◆ Taste
- ◆ Sight
- ◆ Smell
- ◆ Hearing

Our psychic introduction begins with the familiar five of daily life, otherwise known as the five senses. The senses are, quite literally, second nature to us. We don't have to think about using them, we just do. Of the five senses, there is an additional sense that is not commonly thought of in the same group. You might say it is the black sheep of the senses, and it is called the sixth sense. This sixth sense is in fact our psychic sense, which is generally not used with the same regularity as the other senses. This sense is also known as ESP (extrasensory perception). The sixth sense encompasses the many different skills that come under the umbrella word of 'psychic'.

Introduction to psychic senses

Clairvoyance If you can see your spirit guides from across the breakfast table each morning, and have a close working relationship with your Guardian Angel (spirit guides and your Guardian Angel will be coming up in Chapter 4), these are two sure-fire signs that you have the ability of clairvoyance. It is arguably the most talked about and widely recognised of all the psychic abilities. A clairvoyant has the ability to see the spirit guides/ angelic guides around them, and can even see the colours of the aura (which I describe in Chapter 3). They may also see their spirit guides or indeed the colours of the aura as images in their mind's eye. This ability may seem like a rather sensational skill to possess, which is why clairvoyance is often viewed as the glamorous sister of the psychic senses – everyone wants to have clairvoyance. And yet clairvoyance is just one of the many ways of connecting psychically.

Clairsentience Do you recognise the feeling when someone is standing directly behind you? You may not have heard them or even seen them in your peripheral vision, and yet you can sense their presence all around. This is probably the best way to describe an example of clairsentience: the ability of feeling and sensing. A clairsentient will be able to sense when a spirit guide is making their presence known, and will often pick up on this sense through feeling or through their intuition.

In addition, spirit communication often comes through in the form of 'scent', which can be a pleasant or not-so-pleasant experience, depending on what aromas you like. A clairsentient, for example, may suddenly receive the most unbelievable scent of freshly picked roses, or indeed a waft of perfume, which would arrive totally out of the blue.

Claircognizant Could you imagine knowing very specific details about another person, object or place, without having come into contact with them before? This ability is not your mind playing tricks on you; it might well be a particular psychic ability called claircognizance. A claircognizant is able to pick up on information very quickly through mental images and words, and through their intuition. They may only have to look at or touch the object briefly, but are able to suss out facts that could not have come from a quick browse on the Internet.

Clairaudient If you can hear your spirit or angelic guides getting in touch through sound, it is a sign of your clairaudience. The ability to hear spirit/angelic communication will come through either audibly or through words that come into your mind. It is not as streamlined a form of communication as you would have with a friend; in fact, the sound you hear may be hushed, rather like that of someone whispering to you. A clairaudient would eventually discern the difference between hearing spirit/angelic communication, and their own thoughts.

Clairgustant A clairgustant is able to taste varying different flavours without having eaten that particular food. Psychic connection can come through taste sensation and it often comes through entirely spontaneously. Just as we too communicate with taste – we cook a meal for someone we care about to show them how we feel – so taste, interestingly enough, is a form of psychic communication. I know what you're thinking at this moment, ladies, if the taste is chocolate, bring it on.

Additional psychic abilities you may have heard of

Telepathy Hands up all those who can anticipate what their friend is thinking before they have even said it. I know a few close friends of mine whose hands would be raised to the roof right now. Our ability to sense what another individual is thinking is actually quite natural. As is the case with our close friends and family: we know them so well we can often work out what they are thinking just by observing closely, and we probably know them better than they know themselves. There are some individuals, however, who not only know what another person is thinking but can also communicate with them without any words passing between them. The psychic skill of telepathy is the ability to sense and speak without words. It may seem a little far-fetched, even by psychic standards, and yet if our emotional feelings can be detected and understood without words, so too can our thoughts.

Precognition A precognition occurs when a person has a clear intuitive feeling, or indeed a vision, of an event to come. A precognition is commonly experienced by individuals who possess clairvoyance. Although the vision may be on a grand scale, they are often on a very personal level. You may suddenly have an inspiring vision about your future career or a strong sensation someone is about to call you with some important news. Precognitions are hard to define, as they are unique from one person to the next. If you experience one, trust your Higher Self and go with what your gut intuition tells you.

The above may read like a psychic menu – a taster selection of what is on offer for your delectation. You may have even mentally chosen the ability you would ideally like to have. My one word of advice on this subject is to be open to developing your psychic abilities in the way that comes naturally for you. If you try to force a particular skill, you could well be ignoring another for which you have a natural flair; for example, you may have your heart set on developing clairvoyance and yet your ability may be in clairsentience.

You will eventually gravitate to an area that you feel most comfortable with. No psychic skill is more impressive than the other, it's how you use and develop your ability that makes it special and unique to you.

On a personal note, I was able to 'see' very clearly as a child and into my teenage years. I now 'feel' more around me and have much stronger clairsentience than clairvoyance. I don't know why this has happened, it's just the way it goes.

So now you have read about some of the more widely talked about psychic skills, let's get started on how you can go about developing your own ability.

The psychic *you*

Getting in touch with your psychic self is a bit like embarking on a new relationship. It takes time to become familiar with the new person in your life, the same way as getting to know your new-found psychic self. The relationship should always be developed at your own pace, and in the way that feels comfortable to you. It's a continual process of discovery, so enjoy the journey.

The first psychic steps

Psychic work can begin in any number of ways. You may decide you want to learn how to communicate with your Guardian Angel (which, by the way, is coming up in Chapter 4) or perhaps you want to jump straight into the pendulum dowsing exercise (one of my personal favourites). Being the overly protective girl I am, however (friends and family will vouch for my constant 'text me when you get there' pleas), I want to suggest two initial exercises as an important precursor to any type of psychic work.

These two practices are like the warm-up exercises before the big race:

Being grounded

The simple technique of grounding, literally keeps you 'grounded' and balanced throughout your psychic work. Grounding also ensures you keep in touch with the material world (not that you would suddenly go zooming off at 100mph), and prepares you for the altered state that occurs when carrying out particular psychic activities; for example, most psychic exercises involve some form of meditation, which brings about a more relaxed state of mind. Grounding just ensures you keep perfectly balanced throughout.

Grounding

A preliminary exercise to keep you balanced and 'grounded' as you carry out your psychic work.

Also, I think that doing a bit of 'prep' before any psychic work just allows you to create the right atmosphere and to set the mood. It doesn't have to be a complicated ritual, just something that feels comfortable for you. Before you begin grounding, you may wish to light a few scented candles or prepare a playlist of your favourite chill-out songs. Songs can really help with psychic work, just as long as the music isn't too loud or raucous.

Exercise
Grounding

1. Find a comfortable chair in which to sit. For this particular exercise your feet will need to be flat on the floor.

2. Take three deep cleansing breaths: the in-breath through the nose and then slowly exhale out of your mouth. (There are many types of breathing techniques to choose from, but I find the simplest are the most effective.)

3. Close your eyes, and start to imagine giant roots extending from the base of your feet and growing all the way around, securing you firmly in your seat. Imagine the roots are thick and strong like that of a tree, and make them as big as you possibly can. Just allow this image to run through your mind for several moments. The roots can be as elaborate as you like, just as long as you can visualise them keeping your feet securely on the ground.

This quick and easy grounding exercise will only take a couple of minutes, and the more you practise, the more it will become just another part of your routine. It may seem a little strange at first – imagining roots growing out from under your feet has probably never been a part of your daily agenda. It is, however, an important first step that leads us perfectly to the next psychic warm-up, so do keep seated.

Spiritual

Using your imagina
so if you find it trick
try to make the ima
the various exercise
become stronger.

30

2. Keep the image clear in your m
form: see the film of white
feet, until you are, in yo

Once the protective w
out of the visualisa

Your b
hav

Preparatic

The last preparatory
a believer in any kind of psychic work or not, there is absolutely
no harm in a quick protection exercise. Psychic protection keeps
your energy field safe, namely your aura, which I'll discuss in
Chapter 3. Your personal energy, for example, is exposed to
negative vibes all the time – on the bus, out and about in town,
for example – so it is advisable to keep yourself protected so that
you're not picking up on anyone else's stress. You will find that
the more you develop your psychic ability, the more sensitive
you will become to the energy around you.

Exercise
Psychic protection

1. In your current seated position, start to imagine a beautiful white
   light surrounding your entire being. Make the light as big and as
   bright as you possibly can. You can also envisage the white light
   enveloping you in your very own psychic bubble.

ind as you allow the bubble to
ght over your head and beneath your
r imagination, bubble-wrapped.

ite light has been formed you can now come
ion by slowly opening your eyes.

---

ubble of white light is your very own protective safe
n. White light is purifying and keeps those negative vibes at
ay. Negative energy can zap us at any time. And I use the word 'zap' in all seriousness, as that is exactly what negative energy can feel like. We encounter this negative energy all the time, which is why it is a great exercise to incorporate into your daily life. Earlier in the chapter I mentioned how people are often able to sense and pick up on negative energy. When this happens you are under a form of 'psychic attack', which means you are unwittingly picking up on the negativity and stress around you.

A perfect example of this is on a weekend excursion to the local shopping centre. Throughout the day you will be under constant psychic attack from a multitude of stressed shoppers. Surrounding yourself with your own protective bubble will keep their shopping stress away from you, particularly if you are sensitive and able to pick up on other people's feelings easily. Your bubble acts as your own personal knight in shining armour.

Also, if you commute on a train or bus every day, or if you have a friend who does, suggest she tries surrounding herself with the white light. You'll be ensuring you and your friends are going about your day as illuminated goddesses.

Psychic protection

The energetic protection of purifying white light when carrying out psychic work. It often helps to imagine this protective light in the form of a bubble.

How to activate your sixth sense

Getting to know your psychic potential is a lot like learning a new skill. This particular exercise will help you to start to open up your psychic ability in a very gentle way – always the best way to start.

Psychic ability is very subtle, as it relies on you using your own intuition or gut reaction. It helps you to be aware of the difference between an everyday occurrence and when you are having a psychic experience.

Our sixth sense, when trained, can enable us to get in touch with our psychic self.

Using visualisation

Visualising is the first step to working on opening up that psychic link. When we 'visualise' we are learning to see inside our third eye (located between the eyes). As we continually use our third eye through visualisation exercises we will open up our psychic link further.

We visualise all the time, especially when it's a particularly enjoyable image; for example, how many of us have had fantasies over a potential love interest? We can see his or her face in our mind, as if they were right in front of us. We can see their eyes, hair colour, facial expressions and other features about them, even down to the detail on the jacket they always wear. This is visualising. In fact, it is hard not to visualise. If I ask, 'What are you having for dinner tonight?' You have probably already visualised what it is you are planning to prepare or what you expect to eat. The beauty of visualising is that we can develop it further to become a powerful tool for our psychic development.

Third eye

The chakra (one of our spiritual energy centres) located between the eyes. It is your link to all things psychic and, with regular meditation, it can be opened further to help you reach your psychic potential.

Exercise
Visualisation

Find a comfortable place in which to sit or lie down. You may want to prepare a piece of music in the background and dim the lights – whatever it is that allows you to switch off from the world around you. A couple of minutes of grounding and psychic protection will help you to relax and get into the right frame of mind.

    Once you feel ready, the visualisation can begin.

1. With your eyes closed, start to become aware of the space between your eyes, immediately in front of you. This particular area you are focusing on is your connection to your sixth sense, which is also called the third eye (see Chakras, Chapter 3). Keep focused on this area.

2. After a few moments, start to notice what you are seeing in front of you. Can you see any shapes or momentary flashes of colour? If you do see colour, it may not appear vivid, rather more subtle and hazy. The colours you see may be purple and white.

3. If you can see a shape, you may be looking at your third eye, which will appear as an eye shape. It may be open as if looking back at you. If you are starting to awaken your psychic ability it may appear half shut or even closed. The more you practise, the more your third eye will open. Also, the shape may appear subtle at first, but if you have seen the beginnings of the shape, that is a really promising start.

I mentioned the colours purple and white, as these colours are directly connected to our psychic awareness; however, if you saw any other colours, that is a great first step. The colour you saw indicates where you are emotionally and spiritually at this moment in time – see the aura and chakra colour guides in Chapter 3.

Once you feel you have come to the end of the exercise, wind down with the grounding and psychic protection exercise:

Exercise
Wind down

1. Imagine the roots from beneath your feet are keeping you grounded, but start to wriggle your toes and gently rub your hands together.

2. Next, imagine yourself surrounded by your own protective bubble of white light. And then gently start to open your eyes as you bring yourself back into the room.

Another way to ground after a visualisation exercise is to stamp your feet on the ground. It's also good to have a glass of water close by ready to drink when you finish the exercise.

If at first you don't see any colour during your visualisation, don't be disheartened. Visualisation just takes practice, and you will start to see clearer images as you progress.

Visualising not only colours but images in our mind is an important first psychic step. Clairvoyants have the ability to see images and colour in their mind's eye, so the more we practise these techniques, the more we are opening up our own psychic awareness.

Spiritual Goddess tip

Keep a notepad and pen with you when starting your psychic work. It's a good way of keeping a record of any new developments that are happening. It can be a description of how you feel as you carry out a visualisation exercise, and what you experience in those moments. Even if you feel little to begin with, note down what you hope to achieve or what you envisage your experience to be. It will be useful to look back on your journey to see your developments.

Pendulum dowsing

Any exercise that allows you to experiment with the contents of your jewellery box is already a winner in my book. Pendulum dowsing is an age-old practice that is commonly used to find lost

Making your own pendulum

From your jewellery box, find a pendant which you would be happy to use for this exercise, if you happen to have a crystal pendant, all the better – it is a lovely material to use for pendulum dowsing.

You then need a piece of string that extends about 30cm (12 in). Secure the pendant to one end of the string (most pendants will have a small loop where a piece of string can be threaded through and attached).

It's also a good idea to make a pendulum that you'll be happy to use again and again, so choose a material you will enjoy working with; for example, I like working with crystal, and use the same pendant each time I practise.

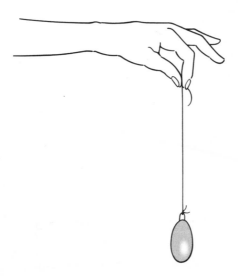

A pendulum

objects, sense energy or even answer your most personal of questions.

How does pendulum dowsing work?

This form of dowsing works by the pendulum picking up on the energy from your subconscious mind – that 'inner' voice that speaks our truth, but which we don't always listen to. It is important to be in a calm frame of mind when pendulum dowsing, as any anxiety or worry will ensure your own Lower Self dictates the outcome. When you let go of worry and concerns, and simply trust in yourself, the pendulum will move naturally to answer your question.

The best way to think of a pendulum is as an extension of yourself, and the pendulum is working on your behalf to give you the honest answer you have been looking for. You can create your own pendulum using items in your jewellery box, all you need to do is follow the simple instructions on page 35.

Exercise
How to start linking with your pendulum 1

1. Start by grounding yourself, then surround yourself with your protective psychic bubble. Once you feel centred and calm, you are then ready to begin.
2. Extend the pendulum in front of you, holding the string between your thumb and index finger.
3. Keep your arm steady so that the pendulum remains completely still.

To begin, you need to establish the responses for your questions. For this exercise we will be working with the basic *yes* and *no* responses. You may be thinking, *How on earth do you start communicating with a pendulum?* The trick is to communicate in the way you would with a friend. There is no kind of psychic speak that you need to follow; simply talk aloud or in your head (whichever you feel most comfortable with). The only difference is that your friend is likely to respond more promptly than a pendulum will.

Working with a pendulum is a form of 'divination', which means working with a psychic tool or instrument to help you connect with your Higher Self, which is your psychic self.

Divination

Using a psychic tool such as a dowsing rod or pendulum to ascertain information about a person, a place, or even yourself.

Exercise
How to start linking with your pendulum 2

1. You can start the exercise by asking the pendulum, 'I would like to know the response for "yes".' If, after a few moments, you find there is no response, simply ask again as clearly as you can. Remember to remain calm, and keep your hand as still as possible, so as not to influence the outcome – the pendulum will do all the work.

2. The pendulum will eventually begin a movement, it could be a subtle clockwise rotation or it could be moving anticlockwise,

swinging back and forth or even diagonally. If you find, for example, that the pendulum is moving in a clockwise direction, after it has completed the rotation ask once again for the signal for 'yes' (or as many times as you like). You want to ensure the pendulum understands the response for 'yes' every time you ask.

If you find your pendulum is being a little stubborn, don't be put off, simply take a break and then start afresh later on. It is an exercise that requires plenty of patience, but you'll soon get the hang of it.

Once you have the signal in place for 'yes', you will then need to ask for the 'no' response. The 'no' response will be different from that for 'yes'. Once you have sussed out the movements, it might be an idea to note them down and draw an accompanying diagram to remind you for next time.

Once the responses have been decided, you can now start asking away. I would suggest keeping the questions nice and simple to begin with. Just remember the answers will have to be a yes or no response.

You may find your pendulum takes a bit of time to get going, or it may respond instantly. It's different for everyone. You and your pendulum will eventually find your own unique rhythm.

Spiritual Goddess tip

The more you work with the pendulum the more you can train it to give you further responses; for example, you may want to ask the pendulum to keep searching for an answer. You can then ask for a response for 'try again'.

Practise with a friend

Using a pendulum is a great exercise to share with a friend – you can take it in turns to observe how each of your pendulums move. The thing to know about pendulum work is that it does take time and practice, so don't be put off if you don't see much at first. Believe me, there have been times when I've almost flung my crystal across the room in frustration. Keep with it, and you'll start to see the results.

'I can see the end coming!' . . . of the chapter, that is

In any discussion of the 'psychic' the question that always crops up is, 'Can you see into my future?' If I had a pound for every time someone asked me that question I would be a very rich woman indeed. And the question I often pose back is, 'Why don't you look for yourself?' The answer they want is already within them.

Psychic ability, to me, has always represented a very personal journey. Learning how to unlock and tap into your own unique ability puts the word 'psychic' in a whole new light.

Your potential is all there for you to discover, so enjoy developing your ability in your own good time and in your own fabulous way. Further psychic exercises will be illustrated throughout the book, so you will find the one that resonates with you the most.

One final friendly word of advice, and something I think you'll carry with you for many years to come: keep away from fortune-tellers with goldfish bowls.

Energy, Auras, Chakras... Oh My!

There is no feeling more frustrating than being completely drained of energy. We've all had that moment when our friend calls us at the last minute to arrange a night at the cinema, followed by drinks, when the only consumption you had in mind for that evening was a mug of steaming hot chocolate to go with the latest reality-TV fix. Please tell me that's not just me!

Our lives are so crammed full of to-do lists and endless daily tasks that by the time 7.00 pm comes around you may be thinking to yourself, *Where did all my energy go?*

When you get an attack of the 'energy drain' it feels as though your personal battery is slowly dying and you're trying desperately to function on the one remaining bar.

Energy is an unusual concept when you start to break it down. Where does it come from anyway? How do you define it? Why do some people seem to have more of it than others? And as our lives get all the more busy, that elusive energy 'fix' is getting harder and harder to find. No wonder we're always reaching for coffee as we go about our day, it's the only thing we know of to keep us going.

It makes you realise we could all probably do with something of an energetic overhaul to help bring ourselves back into perfect harmony – without the need for caffeine.

The aura

Has anyone ever told you that you have a certain 'aura' about you? That indefinable something or *je ne sais quoi* that makes you stand out from the crowd? Being the goddess you are, I'm sure you've received that compliment. This is also the best way to describe the 'energetic' kind of aura you also possess. It is also a seemingly indefinable quality, because the aura isn't immediately visible to the naked eye. Your aura is with you 24/7, and yet we only experience it on a subconscious level, as we're simply not aware of using it.

The aura is, in fact, the energy field that surrounds the human body. It extends for several inches away from your body (depending on your current emotional and physical well-being).

The 'sciency' bit

Just as you are a physical being, you are an 'energetic' one too. This is because the aura is made up of electromagnetic energy, containing seven layers. The outer layers are connected with our spiritual or psychic self, whereas the layers closest to our body are connected to our material world.

Your aura is unique to you so it could not be replicated on any other person. You could liken your aura to your very own shadow, as it reacts in perfect symmetry with how you are feeling on a physical and emotional level. Later in the chapter, I will take you through an exercise on how to view your aura.

The diagram below shows how your aura might look.

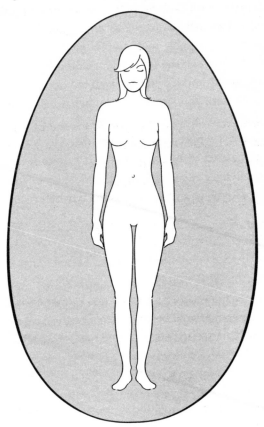

The aura

I say 'might', as it illustrates how the ideal aura would look, which should roughly resemble an egg shape, extending over the top of your head and beneath your feet. The thing to know about auras is that they change constantly and look different from one moment to the next. How we feel alters all the time, as we are exposed to life's multitude of experiences: TV, film, newspapers, books, friends, family . . . every moment opens up an entirely new set of thought processes and emotions, and it is these experiences that shape our aura.

The aura is predictable in its unpredictability. You can guarantee it is changing all the time. If, for example, you have had a disappointing day and haven't felt well in your self, your aura is likely to look dark and sunken – somewhat flat. The aura is in fact reacting to you and how you are feeling. The following day might present a whole new scenario whereby you experience some great news that totally turns the previous day on its head. Your aura will have expanded from this positive change, and will be shining a lot brighter than it was the day before.

Spiritual Goddess tip

Each emotion has a completely different energetic quality from the other, which is why psychic protection is useful to incorporate all the time. Our energy can change so quickly from person to person; one moment we're projecting a relaxed and chilled vibe with our friends, the next we're on our very best behaviour to meet the boyfriend's parents.

Sensing the aura

Energy is constantly affecting us at every moment; everything we do, think or feel is energy, which is why we regularly pick up on other people's emotions. In fact, we are exposed to all types of energy, and this is why protecting our 'energetic' self should become an important part of our daily routine.

You have most likely picked up on someone's aura today without even realising it. Perhaps you were chatting to a friend at lunch, and for some reason, which you couldn't instantly put your finger on, you knew there was something wrong. Your friend probably chatted away as if everything was absolutely fine, she may have even told you she feels great. Call it instinct, call it knowing your friend inside out, but you already picked up on how she was feeling by sensing her aura.

If you have arranged to meet up with a friend who is in need of a shoulder to cry on, you may want to think about surrounding yourself with your trusty protective bubble. Discussing problems with friends is a natural and important part of life; however, during the conversation you would have taken onboard your friends' concerns, and your friend (although unintentionally) has quite literally off-loaded her stress on to you, consequently leaving you drained.

Any exchange involving worry or distress can leave us open to psychic attack, as discussed in Chapter 2, which is why it is important to protect yourself. You could think of your protective bubble as your energetic moisturiser: the barrier that keeps negativity at bay while keeping you protected at the same time.

Aura attraction

Our energy also has the ability to attract people into our lives. In fact, you may already be one of those people who strangers seem to gravitate towards on the train or while waiting for a bus. You may not even be looking for company but they have just responded to something within your energy field, namely, your aura.

It also works in the same way when you feel happy. You simply radiate an energy that comes from within, which people will also notice and pick up on. They may not have seen your aura, or even be aware that auras exist, but what is real is the response we all have to energy.

Spiritual Goddess tip

Next time you feel like the radiant goddess that you are, start to notice how people around you respond. Not to worry, your aura won't attract them like glue, but you may notice one or two extra smiles as you go about your day. It's almost as if the world is humming to your same cheerful tune.

The colours of the aura

The colour of your aura speaks volumes about your current emotional and physical well-being, as well as who you are as a person.

We each have a dominant colour within our aura: our signature colour. This dominant colour will show up most of the time; however, you will also have different colours depending on your current frame of mind. We girls are complicated creatures, after all.

Colour plays an important role in our energetic well-being as it actually nourishes us on a spiritual level. We are always told how we need to incorporate our five fruit and vegetables a day as part of a balanced and healthy lifestyle; colour provides our psychic nutrition, as it feeds us on an energetic level and heals the aura.

For example, you may have experienced a busy week, and feel sluggish as a result. Simply refer to the colour guide below and decide which colour you think will help with your lethargy. White, for example, is a purifying colour, which can assist in clearing negative and trapped energy within the aura.

You can incorporate colour to heal your aura in any number of ways, such as putting a vase of flowers in your room of the corresponding colour. If you were incorporating white, a bunch of freshly cut daisies might be a nice choice. You could even accessorise your latest outfit with a white purse.

By tuning in to how you are feeling, you will be able to look after your aura by satisfying it with the colour of its craving.

Spiritual Goddess tip

To feed your aura, always listen to what your instinct has to say. You may not see the colour in your aura straight away, so learn to rely on your intuition to decide which colour is right for you.

Aura colour guide

Purple is commonly known as the spiritual colour, which is linked to our psychic awareness and the all-important power of intuition. If you are starting to develop your intuitive abilities, which is an important first step in learning about your psychic self, purple may be shown within your aura.

Red This energetic colour signifies a passionate flair and a motivation to get things done. Your vibrancy for life is infectious and you're a person who never goes unnoticed. You consider yourself the leader in whatever you decide to do and are often the person taking charge. You are also interested in material objects and possessions.

Blue This colour represents a balanced point of view and a sense of fairness in all things. You show consideration for all people, and your sensitive nature and reliability ensures you are someone people feel they can trust. You also have the ability to always see the best in others.

Green This 'nature' colour expresses your desire for a loving and harmonious experience. You enjoy nature itself and are most likely the outdoorsy type – the nature goddess, you might say. You appreciate the balance in life and have a very sensitive side, showing kindness and compassion for all people.

Orange This optimistic colour shows your bright and forward-thinking outlook on life. You aim to be inspired by life, and in doing so, are an inspiration to others. Highly motivated and confident, you also convey warmth, which ensures you are someone people always enjoy being around.

Pink is the colour of the all-encompassing feeling that is love. Pink symbolises your love, not only for those close to you but for your fellow goddesses. You show a great deal of compassion, warmth and kindness to everyone around you. The famous saying 'All you need is love' is certainly not lost on you.

Yellow The positive yellow symbolises your sunny outlook on life. You radiate all those joyful, happy vibes that seem to make everyone around you feel good about themselves. You possess a natural joy, which radiates from within. The colour also indicates a fierce intelligence.

White This 'purifying' colour is connected with your spiritual side. The colour shows you are strongly linked to who you are on a spiritual level and feel connected to the path you're on. White is also linked with purity, as you aim to seek the truth in all matters.

The colours of the aura are open to your own interpretation. Use the colour guide as a starting point. Make use of your intuition to detect what the colours mean to you. The more you work with colour, the more you will suss out further what the colours are trying to tell you; for example, you may notice a flash of red within your aura. Think about where you are emotionally at the time. You could interpret it as too much focus on materialistic items; however, red also symbolises your passionate side, so it could also indicate where you currently are with a work project. Always use your intuition to understand what your aura is communicating to you.

We will also be looking further into how colour can enhance our happiness and well-being later in the book (see Chapter 8).

Exercise
How to see the aura

You can do this exercise in two ways. The first, I think, is the most enjoyable as you'll need the assistance of a friend.

1. Find a blank wall in your home, a neutral colour is best. Make sure you can stand flat against the wall, so if any pictures are blocking your way, you may want to make a temporary adjustment. Your friend should find a chair to sit opposite you, about six feet away; alternatively she can stand.

2. While you keep still against the wall, ask your friend to focus her gaze around the top of your head, but not to look directly at you. She will then need to choose a spot to focus on, a few inches away from where your head is positioned.

3. Ask her to focus on that particular spot, allowing her gaze to soften so that her peripheral vision can begin to detect any activity around the top of your head.

4. At first glance, there may appear to be a fuzzy halo effect a couple of inches above your head. What she is detecting is your aura.

If your friend happens to glimpse any patches of colour, ask her to describe how the colour appears. If your friend can't see colour at first glance, not to worry, seeing colour can take time, so just enjoy the experience and remember to swap so that you can have a go at seeing the aura too.

As reading the aura is subtle work, you may wish to take a break at this point. If you can, take a walk outside to refresh yourself before the next step in your aura work.

Exercise
How to feel your aura

1. Place your hands directly in front of you, so that your palms are facing each other.

2. Slowly move them back and forth in a clapping motion, but don't allow your hands to come together. It can be helpful to imagine you have a ball between your hands, which prevents them from touching.

3. Start to sense what it is you are feeling between your hands. Are

your hands warm? Are you experiencing a tingling sensation on your palms or over your fingertips?

4. As you slowly move your hands back and forth, you may notice resistance between them. Can you feel a pulling sensation, as if your hands want to close together? This, ladies, is your aura.

This energy between your hands can feel amazingly tingly, and the more you practise, the more strongly you will feel the sensation. In fact, next time you practise, gradually move your hands further apart and see how far you can feel the energy.

This exercise is great to practise at any time, as it's so easy to do. Why not practise if you're stuck for something to do? You may be on a long train journey and instead of reaching for that magazine why not practise feeling your aura – who knows, you may start a new trend.

Exercise
How to view your aura

For this aura exercise you'll need to find a large mirror in which you can comfortably see the top half of your body.

If you are able to sit for this exercise, all the better, but standing is fine too. I speak a lot about being able to sit when going through the exercises, and the reason is that any work involving the psychic is generally very subtle and often requires periods of concentration, so the more comfortable you are the more you will get out of it.

1. So, now you are sat in front of the mirror, start to observe what is happening around your temples. Make sure your focus is not too intense. Simply allow your gaze to soften and make use of your peripheral vision (what you see around the sides when looking

straight ahead). Move your gaze gently from side to side, not looking directly at the top of your head.

2. After a couple of minutes, you may start to see a soft outline, like a silhouette around your head and shoulders. It may not be clear; in fact, it is likely to look fuzzy. You may, however, detect more, such as patches of colour, but at the start of the exercise the outline is likely to look very subtle.

Just remember, the more you practise the more you'll see.

Spiritual Goddess tip

In all of these exercises, keep your gaze as relaxed as possible. It is also important that you feel calm within yourself, so if you're feeling tired or your next-door neighbour has, rather unhelpfully, turned their TV up to a deafening volume, try this exercise again when you are in a more chilled frame of mind.

Aura maintenance

Looking after your aura is much like the personal grooming we girls tend to do. If we want our hair looking glossy and full of health, we slather on conditioning treatments for some full-on TLC. If we want our aura also looking big, bouncy and full of life, we have to devote the same care and attention. The beauty of the aura is that it doesn't cost you anything to maintain.

A daily aura 'cleanse' can really help improve its condition. Each day we pick up on negative energy, which can linger within the aura. It's therefore a good idea to do some regular aura maintenance to keep it in tip-top condition. It is, quite literally, the same as maintaining your hair, but instead of using a brush you'll be combing through your aura with your hands.

Exercise
Aura cleanse

1. Take both hands over the top of your head (a few inches above, but whatever distance you feel is best) and then move your hands over the front of your face in a brushing motion.
2. Repeat this action around the top half of your body, including the back of your head, shoulders and chest.
3. Once you have brushed over your face, around the shoulders and back of the head, continue down your body until you reach your feet. Try to cover as much as you can – I know the back is a little tricky to reach.

This simple technique brushes away the cobwebs, you might say, and is an easy and effective way of keeping on top of your aura grooming.

Looking after your aura can become just another part of your routine. If you think about it, we look after so many elements in our life – those brand new shoes, for example, are lovingly placed within their very own protective bubble, aka the box they came in.

You can start to think of your aura in the same way, and keep it well protected.

The 'energetic 7', otherwise known as your chakras

By now you are probably starting to wonder how much more could possibly be going on within your 'energetic' self. And on that note, let me introduce you to the chakras.

The chakras act as your very own energetic engine. These spinning wheels of energy are responsible for distributing energy throughout our body and also look after specific areas of our emotional and physical well-being. The wheels keep spinning round and round in a clockwise rotation but, like any machine, even an energetic one, sometimes you find a faulty cog. If one chakra is having a bad day, the rest will suffer also. When your chakras are spinning in unison, it is then that you feel balanced and happy.

The chakras all spin at different rates. The three lower chakras (root, sacral and solar plexus) are connected to our earthly or material side and spin at a much slower rate, while the four higher chakras (heart, throat, third eye and crown) are concerned with our psychic and spiritual side, and spin that much faster.

Of course, it will never be possible to have all seven chakras spinning in perfect unison and a glowing aura that shines like a 100 watt bulb – we live in the real world after all – but the more we consciously work with our aura and chakras, the more we will feel the results.

The chakras look after all our different emotional, physical, spiritual and even romantic hotspots; for example, you have a chakra that is related to your romantic life, and if you feel fulfilled in this area of your life, your chakra will be spinning quite happily with no issues to contend with; however, if you are neglecting your love life or you're going through a rocky time in a relationship, your 'heart' chakra is the area which you will need to focus on to bring it into balance.

Each chakra has a corresponding colour, so refer to the chakra guide overleaf. Once you know the colours of the chakras they may inspire you to incorporate them into your life when you feel a particular area needs a bit of attention.

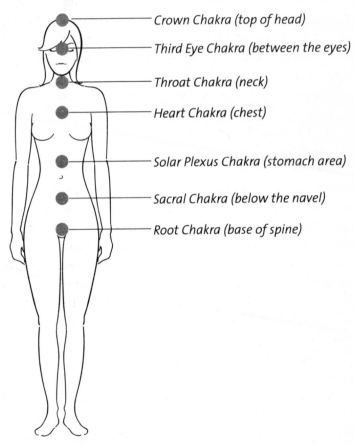

Crown Chakra (top of head)

Third Eye Chakra (between the eyes)

Throat Chakra (neck)

Heart Chakra (chest)

Solar Plexus Chakra (stomach area)

Sacral Chakra (below the navel)

Root Chakra (base of spine)

Where the seven main chakras are situated

Chakra guide

Crown chakra (purple and white) Your link to all things spiritual is through the crown chakra. In Chapter 1 I introduced you to the Higher Self, which is the spiritual aspect of who you are. Everything you truly want to achieve in your life can be linked to the crown chakra. If you have an issue with the direction your life is going, you can trace it back to this chakra.

Third eye (indigo) Your psychic self, or sixth sense, is connected through the third eye. If you regularly use your intuition and are starting to develop your psychic skills, this is the chakra you will be activating. The third eye is how clairvoyants are able to see the aura, chakras and even spirit presences. If the third eye is working well, or if you are just starting to work on opening up your psychic abilities, this is the chakra you will need to focus on.

Throat chakra (blue) All of your communication is connected through your throat chakra. If you are open and honest, your throat chakra will be functioning well. If you have any problems with your communication or feel nervous about communicating what you want in your life, you will need to spend time addressing this chakra.

Heart chakra (pink and green) Ah love! I think we can all agree that this chakra needs constant round-the-clock care and attention. All of our love issues are located in the heart chakra – quite fitting really. If you are nursing a broken heart, be kind to this chakra. If you happen to be 'on cloud nine' in an amazing relationship, this chakra will be making you feel butterflies. This chakra is also related to the love we feel for our friends and family.

Solar plexus (yellow) This chakra is a veritable powerhouse of emotion. Your motivation and will are centred here. Our ambition and drive to succeed are harboured in the solar plexus, as well as many of our deep-seated emotions. If someone is upsetting you, you'll feel that nervousness in your stomach, the same as when you feel passionate about life you will feel that burning desire within to succeed.

Sacral (orange) Your creative side is linked to the sacral chakra. If you have a flair for the dramatic arts or you are wanting to launch into a new project, your creativity will manifest here. Anything involved in creating is directly linked with the sacral. This chakra is also linked with our sexual selves, and our physical wants and desires.

Root (red) The root chakra is connected to our material wants and needs. This chakra is also linked to our survival instinct, so everything that affects us in our daily life – for example, our personal safety, having enough money in our current account, being able to pay off the overdraft – is all tied up with the root chakra.

Seven chakras may seem a lot to look after, and I'm sure I'm adding to your daily list of things to do but, I promise, the chakras are very easy to look after, and the well-being benefits are there to be had. It's all about using our intuition or gut feeling to understand when a chakra needs a little bit of extra care and attention. It works in the same way as taking care of the aura, by being aware when certain aspects of your life need your time and focus.

Chakra maintenance

On a notepad or in your 'psychic jotter' (otherwise known as a piece of paper) write down any issues that have been bugging you of late. I think we all experience those bothersome issues that seem to linger longer than the rest. I find that noting down a problem is a good first step to figuring out where any issue lies.

For example, if you note down that your problem relates to 'motivation' – perhaps you have been putting off getting started on a new project – you can consult the chakra guide to see which area that particular issue relates to. In the case of motivation it would be the solar plexus chakra.

To help bring this chakra back into harmony, try incorporating the relevant colour into your life. In the case of motivation you will want to bring the zesty yellow into your world. If yellow isn't quite your colour of choice, bring it into your home very simply: a bowl of lemons in your front room, a mixed bunch of yellow and orange flowers, a picture in your bedroom containing the relevant colour, and so on. It's all about making small steps to integrate the colour into your life to bring the chakra back into balance.

Also, just by addressing the issue that is causing you concern will prompt you to do something about it. Sometimes we just need a gentle nudge in the right direction to galvanise ourselves into action.

I recently carried out some chakra maintenance on my root chakra, as it was obvious it was becoming out of kilter with the rest of my chakras. I was feeling out of touch with the material aspect of life and wasn't connecting in the way I should. I decided the easiest way to 'feed' this chakra back into better health was to incorporate more of its correlating colour. As it was the root, I started to integrate red into my wardrobe – just simple changes such as a belt, a pair of red shoes, and a slick of red lipstick (a good lippie just makes a girl feel good about herself). I also started addressing the material issues I was ignoring: sorting out my paperwork and texting (my friends will agree I sometimes take a while to text back, but I eventually do).

Chakras

Spinning wheels of energy located throughout the body that are connected to our emotional, physical and spiritual well-being. Everything we think, feel and experience can be linked to a chakra.

Exercise
How to feel your chakras

Feeling your chakras is very similar to feeling and sensing the aura. The chakra you will be working on for this exercise is the heart chakra.

1. In a seated position, place your hand just above your chest, leaving approximately a 30 cm (12 in) gap, and slowly move your hand back and forth, sensing the energy between your palm and your chest.
2. As you slowly move your hand back and forth, become aware of any resistance you may be feeling. Also, you may experience a slight pressing sensation against your chest, which is a sign that you are sensing the chakra.

It can feel very subtle to begin with, but the more you practise the more you will become familiar with the way your chakra feels.

Once you start to feel your chakras, a great next step is to cleanse them, which can become a regular part of your chakra maintenance.

Exercise
Chakra cleanse

A chakra cleanse is very quick and easy to do; in fact, it will take you a mere moment. Of course, you can choose from a variety of different meditative exercises that are on offer, some of which take minutes, whereas others may take up a large chunk of your morning. I like to keep it simple, as you no doubt will have those days where you can barely fit in a lunch break, let alone a chakra cleanse. Also, you don't need to do a chakra cleanse every day, perhaps just on the day when you feel a little low on energy, or if a particular issue is getting you down.

1. Take a quiet moment for yourself, close your eyes, and just imagine a beautiful protective white light, filling your entire being.
2. Allow the light to travel from your crown all the way down the chakras until it reaches the root. Enjoy the visual you are creating, and stay with it as long as you feel comfortable.

White light is purifying, therefore an effective cleanser for the chakras. I think of 'white light' as the detox colour that washes away any impurities and negativity that can get caught within the aura and chakras. Visualising them cleansed and rid of any negative energy will help restore them into balance.

Just a minute or two of chakra cleansing, and you're ready to carry on with the rest of your day. A further chakra exercise is coming up in Chapter 8.

It's sometimes hard to figure out who we are on a personal level, let alone on an 'energetic' one. I think the trick with the aura and chakras is to view them merely as an extension of who you are, and by taking regular care of your emotional and physical well-being, you will be taking care of your aura and chakras too.

Guardian Angels, Spirit Guides and Other Ethereal Observers

Why is it that we are so drawn to angels? Could it be their benevolent force for good, their ethereal beauty and impressive wingspan or the fact that they're ... well, angels? The idea of our very own 'angelic support system' ready to swoop in at our every request is a comforting thought. The angels have our 'back' so to speak, as we navigate this tricky road called life.

It may please you to know that our winged companions are also there to help and support each and every one of us 24/7, 365 days a year, for all our desperate and not so desperate pleas – the 'help me afford the weekend break with friends' being the latter.

I think we can all use a little extra guidance at some point in our lives, the kind of help that is inspired, honest and as pure as the driven snow. I am talking about the kind of help that has no agenda and is coming from the highest place possible: angelic guidance.

The 'angel by your side', otherwise known as your Guardian Angel

If I said you have your very own Guardian Angel with you at this very moment, it may prompt you to take a closer look at your current surroundings. Your Guardian Angel is named as such because they will guide you throughout the course of your journey. Your Guardian Angel is like that fabulous friend who understands all the little quirks and eccentricities that make up the person you are and sticks with you through the best of times and the worst of times. Your Guardian Angel has chosen to be with you, and remain with you, and nothing you can do or say could ever convince them otherwise.

This most closely allied and trusted of guardians also knows where our talents lie, and spends much time moving us towards our true purpose, aka the thing that makes us most happy. Our guardian angels are our inner prompt for when we are on the right path, or, indeed, travelling down the wrong one; for example, if you have ever made a choice that wasn't right for you, your Guardian Angel may send you a number of prompts to help get you back on track. They often communicate these prompts through our gut instincts, so always listen carefully to what your intuition is telling you.

As you start to contemplate your angelic guide as a presence in your life, you will naturally start to imagine what they must look like. Perhaps you view your angel as an ethereal goddess with a mane of fabulous glossy hair? Or, perhaps you view your angel as the down-to-earth person walking next to you in the street? It may be that the traditional image of the cherubic angel sitting atop a candy-floss cloud springs to mind; others, however, may picture their angel complete with huge wings and killer heels. Whatever angel imagery comes to mind, the most important thing to know is that the angels are there for us – in all their fabulous glory.

Angelically speaking, who is with us?

You have any number of angels and guides who are a continual presence in your life, although you may not realise it – think of them as your ethereal support system:

Angels We are surrounded by angels at every moment, and they are here to help us with our every need; all we have to do is ask. Angels can assist us with love issues or career worries. If you need to heal a specific area of your life, there are angels who work in this capacity too. The angels are beings of light, so if you want to invite more winged-companions into your world, it's lovely to light a candle.

Guardian angel Our guardian angel is with us from the moment of our birth, and watches over us throughout the course of our life, and the many incarnations we experience. Our guardian angel records what we do in each lifetime and knows exactly where out true talents and abilities lie. It is this angel who encourages us when we feel we are losing direction, gently guiding us to get back on track. Your Guardian Angel is always with you, whereas angels, archangels and spirit guides move in and out of our lives depending on the type of guidance we need.

Archangels We can call upon the almighty archangels to help us with specific aspects of our life or to help us with areas where we need a more 'bespoke' form of help; for example, Archangel Michael can be called upon for protection and when you need courage and strength, either in a personal issue or to do with your work or career. The archangels watch over our guardian angels and the angels.

Spirit guides This form of guidance differs from angelic guidance, because spirit guides have incarnated on the earth plane before and are not of the angelic realm. You may have a variety of guides with you at any one moment, and you can call upon their help for all manner of issues. They are especially good at practical problems such as finding lost items and helping with work projects.

Angel

An ethereal being of the angelic kingdom who works with us to help us in times of need, and to offer emotional and spiritual support.

Getting in touch with your Guardian Angel

I used to think that to be 'in touch' with my angel I had to be on my very best behaviour at all times and speak in soft, ethereal tones. To be frank, it just wasn't me. My voice is neither soft nor ethereal; in fact, I have been told on numerous occasions to bring it down a notch.

It was a relief to discover that any voice (mine included) could summon the angels for instant angelic chat.

There is no right or wrong way to communicate with your Guardian Angel – you don't have to summon their name three times in some sort of bizarre chanting ritual. Contacting your Guardian Angel should be an easy, fuss-free process that you could do even while running for a bus. But for that initial first introduction, I would advise setting aside a time when you can make it an enjoyable and memorable first meeting.

Signs of angelic communication

- ◆ Tickling sensation on your face, arms or hands.
- ◆ A loving and warm feeling of contentment.
- ◆ White sparks which appear out of nowhere. You may also notice them in your peripheral vision.
- ◆ You may start to see beautiful colour.
- ◆ Angelic guidance through your instinct.

Guardian angel

An angel who is with you from your moment of birth to watch over and record the events of your life. Your Guardian Angel is a most trusted guide, and knows the most important secret of all – your 'true' potential.

Creating your angelic space

To begin, find a quiet spot in your room where you can create your own unique angelic space. An angelic space, quite simply, is an area where you can relax and start to get in touch with your angelic guides. This space is also called a sacred space (see Chapter 7). It also doubles up as the perfect place to flop after a busy day. Start by filling the space with soft cushions, pillows and blankets.

You can also choose to burn incense in the room, as it can create something of a mystical and exotic atmosphere. There are many different types of incense to choose from, and as they are relatively inexpensive, you can always experiment with different scents to find the blend that is right for you. Incense can be quite overwhelming at first, so a good tip is to burn it for 5 minutes prior to contacting your Guardian Angel, and then extinguish the stick just before you start the session. You will then have a gentler aroma flowing throughout the room. (Remember to burn the incense safely away from anything that could accidentally catch light, using a proper incense holder, and never leave it burning unattended.)

The final touch is to prepare a play list of your favourite chill-out songs and, if you like, dim the lights to set the mood even further.

Creating your own angelic space is a great first step to help bring about a relaxed and harmonious atmosphere, putting you in the right frame of mind.

Exercise
Getting in touch with your Guardian Angel

1. Start by taking a few moments to ground yourself (page 28) and apply psychic protection (page 29). (I'm sure by now you have practised these steps several times. The more you do, the more it will become just a natural part of your preparatory psychic work.)

You can sit or lie down when contacting your Guardian Angel, whichever position you prefer.

2. You can now begin the process of contacting your Guardian Angel. Start with a simple 'Hello', and then introduce yourself as if you were meeting a new friend. You can speak aloud, or in your head, depending on what you prefer, and what feels comfortable for you. Although your Guardian Angel knows you very well, this is the first time you have been proactive in establishing the link.

3. You can now request that your Guardian Angel shows you a sign that they are with you. For this, your Guardian Angel will choose to connect in the way that is uniquely right for you.

4. Once you have made the request, allow yourself to be in the moment, and then start to become aware of any change in atmosphere that indicates a sign of angelic intervention.

5. Ask your Guardian Angel to tell you their name. Your Guardian Angel would love you to address them by their name, as it increases the connection between the two of you. This information can be received in any number of ways: as a visual in your mind; you may hear it whispered; it may also come through as the first name that pops into your mind – this will be the name of your Guardian Angel.

6. Thank your Guardian Angel for being with you and then ground yourself (page 28), and start to move out of your current relaxed position. It is always advisable to have a glass of water close by, which helps you to ground further after the exercise.

Once you have made that all-important first link, keep the momentum going by setting aside time every day, or as often as you can, to connect with your Guardian Angel. As you'll already know, the relationships in your life are made stronger over time. The same also applies angelically speaking: the more you nurture the relationship, the stronger the connection will grow.

Build your 'angelic' connection

As you begin to develop your connection with your Guardian Angel you can start to ask more in-depth questions. Here are some examples:

◆ Where do my true talents lie?
◆ How can I achieve my goals?
◆ How can I develop my psychic ability?

Your questions can be anything you want them to be. Your Guardian Angel will be listening, and will find a way to communicate back to you. It would of course be wonderful if our guardian angels made their presence known as soon as we requested, although, if your Guardian Angel suddenly landed on your bed complete with giant wingspan, it would probably give you the shock of your life. Your Guardian Angel doesn't want to scare you and will choose a far more subtle way in which to contact you. One of the most common ways to communicate is through the dreams we have. If you have had a dream that really resonated with you, it may be a sign that your Guardian Angel was speaking to you via the dream.

Your Guardian Angel understands that you may not see them as you go about your day, so the communication often comes through your emotions. You may suddenly experience an overwhelming feeling of pure joy and love, as if you feel at one with the universe. OK, I know these feelings don't occur all the time, particularly at 7.30 am when you're late and can't seem to find your keys. But the sensation of being at peace with everyone around you, and, more importantly, with yourself, is a sign that you are connecting with your Higher Self and becoming attuned to the angelic guidance around you.

Connecting with your Guardian Angel is so simple and enjoyable that it actually feels like a good heart-to-heart with a friend. The only difference is that whereas you will be doing all the talking, your angel will be responding in a far more subtle way. If you cannot see or hear your angel, you will be relying on your intuition.

The sensation you experience when your Guardian Angel gets in touch may feel as though another person has just entered the room. You might not 'see' them, but the atmosphere will indicate that their presence is near. If you happen to have a notepad and pen handy, note down the experience and describe what it is you are feeling. As you become aware of the angelic guidance around you it can be useful to document your experience as a timeline of your development.

Spiritual Goddess tip

You can contact your Guardian Angel at any moment and you will always be heard. It can be useful to vocalise your request; however, if you have a hectic lifestyle and alone time is very rare, your thoughts will be heard just as well.

The white feather, aka the angel's calling card

If you come across a beautiful little white feather, it is a sign that your angel has paid you a visit and left their calling card. A white feather is symbolic of an angel calling, and a personal message to you.

Of course, if you look around your bedroom now, you will probably spy a multitude of items where feathers may be lurking. The feathers from a fluffy duvet or pillow can scatter around the room quite easily. The difference with an angel feather is that you will have an instant emotional response to it, as if it was placed there just for you. The angel feather always offers encouragement and support, and usually at those moments when we need it the most. And if you happen to spy an angel feather, be sure to thank your angel for dropping by.

Where is this angelic/spirit world?

If you go online and type in an address, within a matter of moments you will be shown a visual of your chosen location. You will be given a map, street name, even the neighbouring towns and coffee shops. The certainty of knowing where a place is located is something we are all used to and expect in today's world. And we would, quite literally, be lost without it.

The spirit world is slightly off the beaten track, postcode free and, more frustratingly, isn't even on any known map. I know, it's highly inconvenient for those of us who wish to find out its precise location.

It makes you wonder where the angels, and our other spirit guides, actually call home? I asked myself the very same question when I first started to wrap my head around this very unusual concept of where our ethereal friends lay their heads at night – figuratively speaking.

To break it down, all of us (the spirit world included) are energetic beings, and are constantly vibrating. We are at this very moment. On the 'material' plane – where you and I live – our vibration is at a much, much lower rate, while in the spirit world, they vibrate extremely fast. The reason our vibration is a lot slower is that our physical body slows us down. The angels/spirit guides don't have a physical body to contend with (yes, they all escape the dreaded cellulite!) and are therefore a highly mobile bunch. And whereas it takes us the best part of a morning to travel to meet up with a friend, the angels can journey to any part of the world, day or night, as there are no restrictions on time and space.

The reason we can't see the angels and spirit guides is because they are vibrating too quickly. The spirit realm therefore knows it has to communicate to us in so many other ways, which is why you might suddenly glimpse sparkles of light out of nowhere, or sense a benevolent presence with you in the room, or even a vivid dream that felt as though someone was trying to help you – the spirit world has to be highly imaginative to get in touch with us.

The spirit world could be described as that elusive frequency, much like the reception cover on your mobile phone; for example, have you ever lost the signal on your phone, and then proceeded to spend the next 20 minutes walking around trying to find that perfect spot to recapture it? Getting in touch with the spirit world is a bit like that. At times, you feel so connected and have perfect reception, and at other times, the ethereal connection just doesn't quite . . . connect. We can all learn how to tune into this frequency and get better reception with practice. Regular contact with your Guardian Angel, and visualisation exercises that work towards opening up your psychic link, will strengthen that all-important line of communication.

The archangels

The archangels are a group of highly influential and powerful angels that oversee our guardian angels and the angels. The archangels can offer their highly bespoke form of support for all those big decisions in our lives, as they all have specific areas of expertise. You can match up your request with the archangel of your choice for the perfect angelic fit.

Archangels, like all angels, are androgynous and have both masculine and feminine energies, so it doesn't matter if you refer to them as 'he' or 'she', as it's all related to what resonates with you.

Here is an introduction to some of the archangels on hand to assist you at this very moment:

Archangel Gabriel When you think of contacting an angel, the first thought that may come to mind is *How can I speak to an angel?* You can let that concern simply float away when contacting Archangel Gabriel, who is a powerful and much loved angel for helping us when we are experiencing communication issues. If you find it difficult to put your request into words, simply think it and Gabriel will know that you need some assistance. Archangel Gabriel knows how important communication is to all of us and where our issues lie. At some point along the road we could all do with a bit of extra help in this area, and if you are struggling to express your feelings, Archangel Gabriel will lend a supportive ear and will galvanise into action on your behalf.

On a personal note, Gabriel is the archangel I like to work with on a regular basis. If I have a meeting where I will be speaking in front of several people, or if I'm experiencing a frustrating case of writer's block, I always request Archangel Gabriel to work alongside me to give me that much needed boost of confidence. As soon as I ask for help, I find myself in a calmer frame of mind and find myself working much more productively.

Archangel Gabriel also helps you to find your true purpose.

Archangel Michael Every time I think of Archangel Michael I envisage him galloping towards me on his trusty horse, waiting to obliterate my problem with one mighty sweep of his sword. Phew! It's exhausting just thinking about it. Archangel Michael, you may have gathered, is something of a male protector of the angelic kingdom. The kind of angel you would want around late at night, or in any situation where you feel vulnerable or fearful. Archangel Michael is always on hand to offer his almighty protection, so just let him know when you need his valued assistance.

Archangel Michael also helps with finding your perfect career.

Archangel Uriel Have you ever felt stuck in a rut, or unsure of which direction to take next? It can be a lonely and isolating experience when we veer off our path, as we assume everyone else around us is living their lives to the full and seemingly have it all figured out, which just isn't the case. Always call upon the people in your life to help you work things out and, as an additional option, you can call upon Uriel, who assists those who are wanting to get out of their current situation and transform their lives. Uriel will help you to feel calmer and in a more positive frame of mind, which is when you start to change things for the better.

Archangel Uriel also helps with building your confidence.

Archangel Raphael If you have a beloved pet that hasn't felt quite himself lately, why not send some extra love and healing his way by calling upon Archangel Raphael. One of Raphael's primary roles is to look after animals that are sick, and to provide much needed healing support. With so many of us being animal lovers you can guarantee Raphael's guidance is much sought after. Simply let Raphael know the assistance you need and he will swoop into action. Raphael also provides the healing that you and I need, so if you have a friend or family member who is going through a difficult time emotionally or physically, ask Raphael to send healing energy to your loved one.

Archangel Raphael also helps with healing relationships.

Archangel Haniel Your burgeoning psychic ability can be enhanced even further with the help of Archangel Haniel. If you have recently discovered your psychic spark, Haniel can help strengthen your ability and guide you through your psychic education; for example, you may have started to develop your pendulum work as outlined in Chapter 2, or maybe you're working towards opening up your third eye chakra. Ask Haniel to work with you to support you through your learning and development.

Archangel Haniel also helps with igniting your inspiration and creativity.

Archangel Jophiel Creativity, ideas and inspiration are never in short supply when you invite Archangel Jophiel to work with you. He also helps you to connect with your joyful self, and ensures that you don't neglect your social life. It is the case that when we feel happy and good about ourselves that our creative self is buzzing with ideas. Jophiel wants you to connect with your Higher Self as much as possible, and to help you bring out the happy, free-spirited goddess within.

Archangel Jophiel also helps with clearing away negativity.

Archangel Chamuel The one sure thing we can all count on is relationship issues. We all want the best for our relationships whether it is a friendship or a romantic relationship, and we know that to get the best out of them we have to continually work on them and nurture them. The second we take our eye off the ball is the moment when those 'issues' start to rise to the surface. Archangel Chamuel can be your pre-emptive first strike when you feel a relationship is in need of some TLC. Perhaps you have been arguing with your boyfriend and feel that some kind of divine intervention is needed to stop the bickering. Friendships can also lose their energetic sparkle over time, so Chamuel can help to put the pizzazz back into those relationships.

Archangel Chamuel also helps with bringing balance and harmony into your life.

Archangel Zadkiel Do you ever catch yourself saying 'my hair looks a mess today' or 'I never look nice in anything I wear'? Why is it that we put ourselves down so much? It eventually becomes a naughty little habit, and like any habit, it's often difficult to break. The regular put-downs we think nothing of can eventually become detrimental to our self-esteem, so if you ever catch yourself on the verge of uttering a negative phrase, why not call upon Archangel Zadkiel to help break the cycle. Zadkiel deals with breaking down our negative patterns and will help make sure you're focusing on all your lovely positives.

Archangel Zadkiel also helps with learning to forgive.

If you have an issue which hasn't been listed, simply state your request and ask that an archangel be with you.

You can call upon the archangel's guidance at any time of the day or night – office hours don't apply in the angelic kingdom.

You may finish your day at 5.30pm but an angel's work is never done, and that's just the way they like it.

Whether you choose to call upon your Guardian Angel, archangel, or both, no problem or worry will ever go unheard. And never think that a problem is too trivial or silly for the angels to deal with. They want you to get in touch.

Spiritual Goddess tip

If you are able to pick up on the energy of your angelic guides you may occasionally feel overwhelmed by their presence. If you clearly sense your angels standing too close, you can ask them to kindly step back. They won't be offended, I promise.

If you start to regularly link with the same archangel, you may discover that you enjoy their particular energetic presence. If you find this is the case, there is no reason why you can't request their permanent assistance. And then if you decide you no longer require them by your side, you can simply ask them to leave.

Spirit guides

On a more day-to-day basis, you may find it useful to call upon a spirit guide for assistance. Your Guardian Angel and archangels are very good with the big life decisions we all face, whereas the spirit guides have a particular knack with our more material concerns.

A spirit guide is an entity who has previously lived on the material plane and knows the things that worry and concern us right now. I think we all have a permanent list in our head of familiar issues that bog us down, including the daily 'Where did

I put my mobile?' dilemma. Spirit guides love helping us with our more mundane daily issues, because they too have dealt with these types of problems before. Of course, you can always ask your Guardian Angel for help with this, but spirit guides are particularly good with lost objects and more everyday practical concerns.

One of the more popular requests spirit guides are known for is finding that elusive parking space. In fact, I have tried out this theory many times, and you know what, it actually does work. You don't even have to be a driver, you can be a passenger. If you happen to be heading towards a location which you know is pretty bad for parking, ask your spirit guide to help find a space approximately 20 minutes before you anticipate your arrival. You only need ask once, and just remember to say a polite thank you. Good manners are universally accepted.

How to work with your spirit guide

It can be very helpful to keep a spirit guide close by while you are working on a specific project. If you are studying for a qualification, for example, and you have a long intensive period of study, you can request spiritual assistance for motivation and to help strengthen your creative ideas. You can ask your spirit guide to stay with you for the duration of the project and then ask them to leave once you have fulfilled your task. You don't have to worry about offending your spirit guide, because guidance comes in and out of our lives all the time. Once the spirit guide has fulfilled the task, their work is done.

You will always have your Guardian Angel with you, while spirit guides change like the seasons. You can have as many or as few with you as you so choose. The choice, as always, is entirely yours.

If you wish to start working with a spirit guide, why not think about an upcoming project or task with which you feel you could do with a little bit of extra help. It could be anything from organising your friend's surprise birthday party to upcoming exams; anything where you feel you need that spark of inspiration. At times like these, we have to rally our spiritual cheerleaders.

Linking with your spirit guide

Find a quiet time when you can start a dialogue with your spirit guide and talk about what it is that you require. Try to be as specific as you can, but you only need to ask once. On a personal note, I remember when I first started linking with my spirit guide, I would repeat my request at least four times a day. I would say it in my head, out loud and while on the bus, and then one day my friend turned to me and said, 'They heard you the first time!' She was absolutely right. From that moment on, every time I was on the verge of repeating my request, I heard my friend's valuable words of advice echoing in my head from all those years ago. I think she was acting on behalf of the spirit guides – they must have tired of my constant repetition.

Once you have found that tranquil place where you won't be disturbed, go through the preparatory exercises of grounding (page 28) and psychic protection (page 29). And once you feel totally calm, ask that you receive the highest form of spirit guidance. This part is important, ladies, as the spirit realm is a pretty big place; therefore, you can access all kinds of spirit guides and you only want the very best. It's just like in the material world, we have some fabulous people and some not so great people. Requesting only the highest form of guidance will ensure your guides will be top notch.

You then need to explain what it is you require and go into as much detail as you can. You can even ask for a 'spiritual tag team' so to speak. If your task is particularly creative, you may wish for Archangel Gabriel, whose many areas of expertise includes helping improve our communication. You may also request a spirit guide who specialises in a particular creative discipline. In effect, you are bringing together a spiritual entourage to help you achieve your goal.

For any issue, professional or personal, there is always a guide or angel that can help. And don't be shy whatever your concern, even if it's of an intimate nature – they've heard it all before.

You can even ask that a spirit guide watches over your pet while you are away on holiday. Of course, you will still have to ensure that a friend or neighbour watches over them daily (spirit guides are not adept at sorting the food!) but in terms of spiritual support, spirit guides are very happy to help. The spiritual realm has no constraints of time or space like we do. It's hard to imagine that the spirit guide who is helping you in your project can also watch over your pet, and even your friend on the other side of town. Once we realise this, however, we become comfortable in being more proactive in asking for help when we need it.

Your spirit guide will communicate to you in the way in which you are able to understand. If you are clairvoyant, a spirit guide may appear to you as a person like you or me. You may wonder how you would be able to tell the difference; in fact, you would know instantly as the people around you would not be able to see your spirit guide, unless they happened to have ability in clairvoyance. Also, spirit guides won't interact in the same way as a friend would, so it is unlikely they will sit next to you to flick through the latest weekly glossy! Generally speaking, a spirit guide will communicate through your intuition, which is on a far more emotional and sensory level. When your spirit guide communicates in this way, you may notice a change in atmosphere as they come close to you. It may feel as if another person is in the room with you. You may also receive images or ideas when you dream at night. Spirit communication is subtle, so be on the alert for the signs.

The 'are they watching me wax?' dilemma

I know what you're thinking, ladies, as I too have asked myself the very same question, 'Does my angel/spirit guide see me on the toilet, when I'm kissing my boyfriend, etc?' It's easy to imagine our spirit guides pulling up a few ethereal chairs, armed with popcorn while we wax our legs. I want to put your mind at rest. Although our ethereal companions do have a close working relationship with us, they are not that close, so please don't adjust who you are in your own private time. We all have our 'secret' little activities that we do in the privacy of our own room: plucking our eyebrows, examining our split ends, singing into our hairbrush. The list goes on, does it not? And not forgetting the occasional expletive that slips out as we pull on that wax strip!

Spirit guide

A spirit entity that has previously lived on the earth plane. Our spirit guides assist us with our very human, everyday issues.

Animal guides

The spirit realm may seem like a big place, housing all of our many and varied guides. The guidance on offer is not limited solely to spirit and angelic guides, but also encompasses the majestic guidance of the animal guides.

How to recognise the animal guide working with you

- You dream of the same animal repeatedly.
- The animal regularly pops into your mind.
- You read about the same animal in newspapers, magazines and in books.
- In discussion with friends, the same animal keeps cropping up in conversation.
- You may feel a presence around you and can detect the nature of the animal.

Animal guides are similar to spirit guides in that they offer us assistance with our daily lives and help us with the tasks we are presented with. The only difference with this form of guidance is that the animal will choose the person they wish to guide, much like a guardian angel. You will most definitely have a connection with the animal that has chosen to work with you. In fact, your animal guide is most likely to be the animal you most admire or feel a strong affinity with.

The best time to get in touch with your animal guide is while out and about in nature, so if you are planning an afternoon in the park, that would be the perfect time to get in touch; however, always choose the location where you feel most comfortable.

The animal that has chosen to work with you will be able to offer you a very personal and bespoke form of guidance which suits you as an individual. The animal may share similar traits to you, and has chosen to work with you, as they are able to bring out certain aspects of your personality and help you in certain areas of your life that you may struggle with. Animal guides also help to empower and strengthen us emotionally.

Exercise
'Meet your animal guide' visualisation

This is a really enjoyable exercise as you become the creator of your own visualisation. For this exercise, you may wish to continue with the nature theme and choose to carry out the visualisation outdoors. Of course, if that is not possible, find a location where you feel comfortable and won't be disturbed.

Once you have chosen your perfect spot, you can begin your visualisation.

1. Start with a few moments of grounding (page 28) and apply the psychic protection (page 29) – it's your cosmic moisturiser.
2. Once you feel relaxed, start to create a visual image in your mind of your perfect 'nature' setting. You may wish to envisage yourself on the perfect sandy beach, in a lush forest, or even in your favourite park. Create an image in your mind in which you would enjoy spending some time.
3. Now you have the image in your mind, spend a few moments setting the scene. Can you see people? Is it warm? Can you feel a breeze? What time of day is it? Create the image as you would a painting, adding as much or as little as you like until you feel happy with it.
4. Find a spot in your visualisation where you can sit. Perhaps you have visualised yourself a bench, or maybe you have taken shade under a tree.
5. Once you have found the ideal spot, ask your animal guide to make their presence known to you, and remember to say thank you once you have made the request.
6. Try not to force or create the image of the animal guide that you

envisage having; simply stay focused on where you are sitting and allow your animal guide to come to you.

7. If you sense that they are making their presence known, make them feel welcome with a friendly 'Hello'. They may also be making their presence felt through sound or via a visual image. As your animal guide moves forward, allow yourself to be in the moment and just enjoy the experience. You don't have to make any grand gestures, just remember that this is the first meeting and you'll have plenty of time to get to know them.

8. Once you feel you have come to the end of the visualisation, bring yourself back into everyday awareness by grounding.

This visualisation can be repeated as many times as you like. The more you practise, the more you will connect with your animal guide.

If you have 'seen' or 'sensed' your animal guide with you, that is a great start. You may not see your animal guide as a visual; you may have sensed their presence, or even heard their particular sound. It is always different for everyone. Keep practising this exercise and your animal will make their presence known to you in good time. It is a special relationship, so I promise it's worth the wait.

As you develop your connection with your animal guide, start to ask further questions and see how your animal guide chooses to respond. Here are some sample questions:

◆ What is your name?

◆ Why have you chosen to guide me?

◆ How can I learn from you?

I'm sure you have already thought of many questions you would like to ask, and do feel free to pose them to your animal guide. You may not hear their response audibly, however. As you already know, spirit communication comes through in many other ways, so it might be an idea to keep a journal of any significant dreams, ideas or emotions that come through when you sense your animal guide is communicating with you.

On a personal note, I find there is something so magnificent about animal guidance. I feel they inspire so much love and admiration that it feels very special when they choose to connect with an individual in such a personal way.

I'm sure by now you are wondering which magnificent creature has already picked up on your fabulousness. Of course, there are so many animals I could do a separate book on the many special tasks they can assist us with. I hope the list below will resonate with you, and set you on your path to discovering your animal guide:

Dog If you happen to have the dog as your animal guide, you have a very special animal companion indeed. We all know dogs are faithful and loyal animals, and that translates to their spiritual guidance too. Their unwavering kindness, devotion and gentle temperament is reflective of the people they choose to guide. The dog can teach us patience and unconditional love, and will guide with kindness and dignity.

Cat The magical goddess in you may have attracted the feline companion. The cat symbolises the supernatural powers of the universe, and if you have started on your spiritual journey or have a natural affinity for the psychic, the cat is a trusted and most intuitive guide. The cat is also known to help guide those who are fearful of change, and will help you make the necessary adjustments with new-found confidence.

Bear The powerful bear exudes tremendous physical power and yet has much to teach us about inner strength. The bear helps those who wish to understand more about who they are and what they are here to do. The bear shows the importance of looking inwards for the answer, and listening closer to our Higher Self. The strong and reassuring presence of the bear ensures you work steadily towards your goals with the kind of confidence that only comes from listening to your true self.

Horse The wild spirit of the horse will be drawn to the wild spirits of the material plane. The horse understands your need for freedom, and to play by your own rules. As a goddess who knows her own mind, you journey through life with a restless and highly independent spirit. You also have a tendency to bolt when the people around you become too close. Your horse companion is able to tame, as well as encourage and nurture, your individual spirit.

Dolphin The playful dolphin can teach us about the simple pleasures in life. Fun and play are integral to our well-being, and the hard-working goddess should take heed of the dolphin's wise guidance. Take time to enjoy the activities that make you truly happy – a life without a bit of fun and wild abandon is a dull one indeed. The dolphin will guide you towards a more fun-loving and harmonious experience.

Lion The powerful lion guides and protects those who find themselves harbouring anger and resentment issues. It can be difficult to manage such difficult and powerful feelings, and yet the lion can guide you on how to release the anger from your life, and feel happier and more content with yourself. The calm lion can also help us to deal with difficult situations more peacefully so we keep our head and still retain our power.

Wolf The loyal wolf can teach us about our own personal needs, and also how to work more closely with the people around us. The interesting thing about the wolf is that he may choose to appear to you alone, or in a pack. If you spy a lone wolf he may have come to teach you about 'self-love' and how to nurture yourself. If you happen to see or sense a pack of wolves with you the guidance may be focused on helping you to work more closely with your friends and family, and emphasising the importance of nurturing those relationships.

Owl The quiet and introspective goddess may have attracted the soulful qualities of the owl. Your calm and considerate nature indicates a wisdom beyond your years and you may spend a great deal of time observing those around you. The owl will gently guide you towards a career path that reflects your unique skills and ability.

Tiger New challenges are afoot when the tiger pounces into your life. The tiger loves an adventure and wants you to embrace opportunity and change in your life. Tigers are also strongly linked with the psychic, and guide those who have a natural or burgeoning ability in this area. The tiger will always keep you on your toes and will open up the passion you never thought you had.

In that eternal quest to understand who we are, and where our true talents lie, it often falls to someone close to us to prompt us into acknowledging how much we are truly capable of. Our guardian angels, spirit guides and other ethereal observers want to help us fulfil that potential too.

All around you, a legion of spiritual helpers are at your side who all have front-row seats to the journey that is 'your life'. In many ways they are your most ardent and loyal fans, who have supported you right from the very beginning, willing you on in whatever makes you most happy. And although you may not see them in the conventional sense, you can be sure they will be with you, every step of the way.

Manifesting: More than Just a Flick of a Magic Wand

I once had a pair of ruby-red shoes that possessed a very special and magical power: with three clicks of my sparkly heels I would be transported to a fantastical land of make believe. I reasoned that if it worked for Dorothy from the *Wizard of Oz*, then surely it could work for me too. As you can imagine, after forcibly clicking my heels any number of times, I was still in the land of the untidy bedroom rather than the magical land of Oz. Oh well, we can dream can't we?

Our innermost wishes and desires never quite lose their magical sparkly quality, do they? Even if we push them right to the back of our minds, locked in the vault of make-believe, they somehow manage to pop up during those idle moments when we remember all of those exciting adventures we dreamt up for our future. As we grow up, our wishes change somewhat (I no longer covet the princess castle complete with all the furnishings) and our childhood whims and fancies are replaced by more 'grown-up' aspirations. These new dreams become an intrinsic part of who we are and give our lives that all-important focus. Our dreams take the shape of potential love interests and career or personal goals.

Transport yourself back to a period in your childhood when every moment held a brand new possibility for you. Sift through the memories to a dream which always took a very special place in your heart. Think about that dream now, and ask yourself if it is something you still feel passionate about. Of course, any dreams involving ruby-red slippers, magical lands and talking scarecrows, are reserved for that all too fleeting childhood, but not all our dreams are the stuff of make-believe. Some dreams are capable of actually coming true.

You may wonder, *How do you then turn that dream into a living and breathing reality?* If we all possessed that magical wand, wouldn't life be so much simpler? But in lieu of a wand (and a pair of ruby slippers) let me introduce you to something a little more fitting for the 21st-century goddess.

Manifesting – the process revealed

For all you dreamers out there, I say never give up on the dream. I hand-on-heart believe that if you have a goal which you have secretly harboured for as long as you can remember, you must pursue it with every fibre of your being. If you set your 'intention', you can accomplish anything. And that's not just the eternal optimist in me. I think we are all capable of so much more than we give ourselves credit for.

Years ago, I heard about the process of 'manifesting': a universal delivery service of sorts, which aims to bring about that which you desire, once a simple request has been put in. As soon as you have set your all-important intention, the 'wish' will find a way to manifest into your life. *Does my request also arrive at my front door before 9.00 am the next day?* I wondered. This was surely too good to be true. I soon discovered the invisible small print at the bottom reads that we also have to do our fair share of the work to make our dream a tangible reality.

The first thing you need to know about manifesting is what I like to call the 'sciency' part of the process. Manifesting works on the energy we give out to the universe. Everything we think and feel has an energetic quality to it, and when we daydream or visualise a goal, we are effectively creating a template of what it is we wish to accomplish. By focusing positively on what it is we want, we will attract positive results like a magnet. We may not see the energy around us, and yet we will tangibly feel the results. Try this mini experiment and see what happens: spend a day thinking positively, making sure your actions reflect your optimistic attitude, and notice the happy and positive vibes that are reflected back.

Spiritual Goddess tip

Manifesting is not a new concept by any means; in fact, it is something you are already utilising in your life right now. Anything you have created or achieved has been manifested by you.

Step-by-step guide on how to manifest

Before the process can begin, you need to have in mind what it is you would like to manifest. It doesn't have to be on a grand scale: perhaps you want to manifest a short-term goal, such as the financial means to buy an outfit you've had your eye on for some time. Alternatively, if you are setting your sights on a particular career path, you may want to start the manifesting process now to move the process along, bringing you closer to your chosen goal.

Exercise
Step 1 – what do you want?

1. Find a quiet space in your home or outdoors where you can relax and you won't be disturbed. The first step involves finding out about what it is you really want. Have a series of probing questions in mind to help clarify your aim:
   - What do I really want to achieve?
   - What steps do I need to take to make my dream a reality?
   - How will I feel when I achieve my goal?
   - How will my friends react when I tell them?

   Delve deep, know it by heart, so you have no doubt in your mind as to what it is you are aiming for.

2. Allow yourself to start the 'visualisation' process. It's free rein to daydream, ladies. Enjoy the visual you create, and see your goal in your mind's eye – be specific with the sights, sounds and smells as if you are experiencing them in real time. Your visual is your very own blank canvas to do as you please. Add as many colours to your picture as you want, and also discard the images you don't want to use. Don't hold back either; this is your dream and only you and the universe need know.

   In your mind, you are creating a little movie, and while it may seem silly to anticipate a moment that hasn't actually happened, it is important that you are able to visualise what it is you desire. Allow yourself to feel excited, even down to how your friends will react when you tell them your exciting news.

3. The universe needs to hear, either aloud or in your head, what it is that you desire. The brilliant thing about manifesting is that you only need to ask once. I always advise asking out loud, as it reaffirms exactly what it is you want to achieve.

4. Start a manifesting book to record the moments when you feel particularly inspired or when you pick up on any clues that indicate the manifestation is coming into fruition. You may have a flash of inspiration while travelling on a bus, while walking in the park, or even taking a bath. Ideas often hit us when we least expect them and when we're not trying too hard, so keep that book handy at all times.

Spiritual Goddess tip

To help the visualisation process you may find it easier to close your eyes. I always think it helps with concentration.

The universe will bring about a series of prompts and signals. They may not be immediately obvious to you, so keep alert for the signs:

Synchronicity Have you ever thought of a friend who you haven't heard from or spoken to in ages, and a day or so later you bump into them unexpectedly on the street? If so, you have experienced a synchronistic event. As soon as you begin the manifesting process you will start to see more synchronicity occurring in your life. One of the common synchronicities people experience is the out-of-the-blue telephone call: you think of a person and the next moment you receive a call from them. As soon as you give your energy to a person – or indeed a thought – the universe starts to move into action to bring you what it is you desire. Be open to the twists and turns of fate, and the new opportunities that move you closer to your goal. If, for example, you receive an invitation to an event or party, just say yes and see what a new experience will bring. Seize as many opportunities as you can. Life has a funny way of bringing us more abundance when we also make the effort.

Dreams Have you ever woken from a dream that was so vivid that it stayed with you? Most dreams diminish from our thoughts shortly after we wake; however, some dreams seem to leave a lasting impression that affects us on an emotional level. If you start to experience a repetitive dream, or you feel you are being given clues with regard to your request, make a note of your dream as soon as you wake. Our dreams are symbolic of our feelings and hidden wants and desires; they also inspire and help us with our dilemmas. Our guardian angel also communicates with us through our dreams, guiding us towards the path that makes us most happy. Now is the time to be sleep savvy, ladies.

Friends If you are happy to share your dreams with friends or a family member, all the better. Vocalising what you want can help bring you closer to the result, as it reinforces your goal. We often disguise our dreams even to our closest friends for fear of what they may think, and yet those closest to us often have a few veiled wishes themselves. I have yet to meet a person who doesn't harbour a secret wish and, maybe, if they confided in the people around them, it might inspire them to take that important first step. Also, your friends might have some fresh ideas on how you can go about pursuing your dream. Two heads are better than one, I always say.

Intuition How do you describe a moment when you just 'know'? It is an instinct that cannot be explained, and has no set pattern or logical reasoning, and yet we have all experienced our inner prompt or 'intuition'. You may experience it as a feeling in the pit of your stomach, it could even make the hair on the back of your neck stand on end, but that all-encompassing feeling of 'knowing' is something we sense in our own individual way. Intuition is your Higher Self making its presence known to you in a very stomach-fluttering sort of way. It can be a really emotive experience, so listen carefully to this powerful form of inner communication.

Exercise
Step 2 – making your dream happen

1. Think about the steps you now need to take in order to make your dream a reality. The manifesting process is a bit like a tag team between you and the universe: you work together to make the process work. Our goals generally take some form of logical step-by-step route, so by sitting down and taking time to map out those small steps, you will eventually be making large strides towards achieving your goal.

2. Keep positive, keep momentum! You may now be wondering how long it takes for your wish to manifest. In truth, it all depends on the type of request you have, and how much you are willing to work towards achieving it. From the moment you set the request, it is important to stay positive and persevere. If you feel your focus slip at any time, refer back to the second step of the first part of the manifesting process – the 'movie' clip – and run your dream through your mind to feel inspired again. If your dream still makes you feel goosebumps, it is a sure sign that it is a goal worth fighting for.

The ultimate wish list

It's my 'sad' little thing, but I simply love making lists. I can't get enough of them. That little piece of paper scribed with my most pressing of objectives has the potential to set my pulse racing faster than the sight of a brooding Robert Pattinson. You may wonder at this point if I need to get my priorities straightened out, and you know what, I have a list for that too.

The reason I bring up the list is that manifesting requires careful and precise consideration of what it is you actually want. Creating an ultimate wish list is ideal for all those dreams and ideas you have that are just simmering away. The simple act of writing down the wish can give that goal its first breath of life. It is also a helpful precursor to the manifesting process, particularly if you haven't got your wish all figured out in your mind, and you need to build up a clearer picture of what it is you want; for example, your big dream is to have a successful career earning loads of money – a perfectly acceptable ambition, granted, and certainly one worth manifesting – but if the details (if I can call them that) are so vague, it doesn't give the universe much to go on.

By sitting down and putting pen to paper, you can start to flesh out the plot of your story, aka your dream. Write down the goal, but also note down the steps you need to take to go about making it a reality. Writing this list may prompt you to start making progress now. Perhaps enrolling in an evening or weekend course may help you get on that first rung of the career ladder, or maybe the first thing you have noted is to speak to someone in the field you would like to work in. This list can become a real source of comfort to you, as we all need a little reminder of where we are going and the steps we need to take to get there.

I keep my wish list on my bedside table, and refer to it at least once a week to reinforce my goals.

Spiritual Goddess tip

The phrase 'be careful what you wish for' is very apt when it comes to manifesting. Be careful when asking for what you want – you just might get it.

Pretty, pretty thoughts

Your thoughts are an incredibly powerful tool, and can be harnessed to maximise your manifesting potential.

Our thoughts can change in an instant from positive to negative; this often translates as very confused messages to the universe. The more you can keep your thought patterns upbeat and optimistic, the better – whatever we give out, comes right back, after all.

I realise that having perfect, pretty thoughts about everything and everyone all the time is a big ask. But being the goddesses we are, we endeavour to keep the more spiritual perspective on life – we try anyway. And our thoughts, with practice, can be disciplined in order to attract more of what we truly want.

The problem with a negative thought, worry or concern is that it has the tendency to stick with us. The more we hold on to the negativity, the bigger it escalates. Become more aware when an issue arises and catch it before it grows out of control. Next time you are feeling in a negative mood, visualise the emotion and then imagine that negative energy trapped inside a bubble from which it can't escape, and simply allow it to float away out of sight.

Visualising our concerns can help us to then release them from our lives. Of course, any residual feelings of frustration and negativity won't disappear just like magic, but cutting the cord between you and the negative emotion is a step towards focusing your energy on the things that really matter to you. I think us girls, in particular, hold on to a lot of negative energy and it often gets in the way of our general happiness and well-being. Just imagine how much more room there would be in your life for all the good and positive once the negative is removed.

Paying more attention to our thoughts can ensure we are sending out only the good stuff to the 'movers and shakers' of the universal cosmos.

Spiritual Goddess tip

As you start to manifest, you may worry that you won't pick up on all the signals; please don't fret about this, as it's virtually impossible to stay on high alert all the time. The universe will continue to present you with opportunities.

Manifest the 'right' path

I do truly believe that we can get what we want when we are choosing the path that is right for us. I think we all have a fair idea of where our abilities lie, and what we'd be good at. By comparison, we also know the no-go areas. For me, that hazardous no-go area is singing – not a skill I have ever mastered.

I came to the disappointing conclusion one Christmas after belting out a 'tune' and watching the tape back when I had said, 'It must be the camera making all that noise.' My friend, on the other hand, is an amazing singer and could start manifesting right now to bring about the opportunities to help her with her career.

I resign myself to singing (poorly) in the shower, and put my energy towards the areas where I feel I can thrive. There is nothing more satisfying than setting your sights on an ambition where you know you can achieve something – a far more exciting prospect than pursuing an avenue which just isn't right for you.

We all have a talent, and we are all capable of developing skills. It's just about finding the one that is uniquely right for you. I think it's about time I (begrudgingly) packed my microphone away.

How do I figure out my path?

Figuring out what to do with our life is not always an easy task. At times, it may feel like we have a huge question mark hanging over us, and can make us apprehensive about our future and uncertain of which road to take next. I have found there is no right or wrong choices when it comes to your career, it's just a matter of figuring out what makes you happy.

At moments such as these it can be useful to practise an exercise called 'automatic writing'.

What is automatic writing?

Automatic writing is a form of 'channelling'. Channelling is the process of receiving spirit/angelic communication through your intuition, where words and even images suddenly spring to mind. Channelling is most often called upon when you need some much-needed creative inspiration. It can also happen spontaneously at any moment, so do keep a pen and paper handy. Alternatively, you can set aside a time to actively channel.

The process of automatic writing can help you figure out the answers to those burning life questions we all have, and even inspire you to find out your higher purpose. For this exercise, we will be channelling from our Higher Self. The exercise works by allowing thoughts and ideas from your Higher Self to flow through during the writing session. The process works by taking what you want or *feel* you should write out of the equation, and allow the words and wisdom to come from your Higher Self.

Exercise
Automatic writing

1. Find a comfortable chair and table where you have plenty of room to write. All you require is a few sheets of A4 paper and a pen – it's always a good idea to have some paper spare. Also, ensure you remove any chunky bracelets that may constrict your flow of writing.
2. Start by grounding (page 28) and then surround yourself with your protective bubble (page 29), which ensures you are balanced before you begin the exercise. It will also help to put you in the right frame of mind so you get the most out of the exercise.

3. Once you feel ready to start, take a moment to think about what you want to get out of the automatic writing session. It can be useful to pose a question to yourself such as 'What do I want for my career?' 'Where do my talents lie?' or 'What career will inspire and fulfil me?' You can think the question to yourself or out loud. You can even ask your Guardian Angel for inspiration – all you have to do is ask.

Spiritual Goddess tip

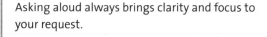

Asking aloud always brings clarity and focus to your request.

4. Put pen to paper and write what immediately comes to you. It often helps not to look directly at the piece of paper – don't worry about your handwriting, as this is not a competition in neatness. It is important not to write what you feel you ought to write, but what is instinctively coming to you at that very moment, almost as if the pen is writing of its own accord. It may not make any immediate sense to begin with, and you may only receive a few random words or pictures, but whatever comes to you, just make a note of it. The more you practise, the more you will receive and the writing will really start to flow. You may also notice your style of writing changing throughout the exercise; for example, you may have the urge to write in very large letters or perhaps smaller than usual – just let the process flow organically.

5. The most important aspect of automatic writing is not to analyse what you are writing. Remember, it is being channelled from your Higher Self, or spiritual self, so it may sound or feel different from how you may write on a day-to-day basis.

6. Once you feel you have come to the end of the exercise, take a few moments to ground and then surround yourself with your protective bubble again.

7. Take a look at what you have produced. You may have received a sentence, a paragraph, or perhaps a few words or even symbols. There is no right or wrong answer, and it doesn't matter if you didn't receive anything, as it's all a matter of practice. If you did receive information, take some time to think about what it means to you. It may not be immediately clear, but when we channel from our Higher Self it is guidance in the purest form.

As you keep practising, you will find the writing sessions will become longer. At the beginning, 5–10 minutes is all you need to get comfortable with the process.

Automatic writing should be an inspiring and enlightening experience, so do keep with it until you find the answers you are looking for.

Spiritual Goddess tip

If you find you no longer wish to pursue a particular goal, remove your energy from it and focus on your new objective.

Affirmations

It is my belief that personal affirmations are in need of a big comeback. We ladies are certified professionals when it comes to giving out compliments, and yet we often play down or ignore our own self-worth. It's often left to our friends and family to remind us of all our lovely qualities, and to give us that much needed 'big up'. And yet, paying ourselves a daily compliment or affirmation can just as easily become part of the daily routine.

An affirmation is a positive statement designed to boost confidence and reaffirm the fabulous person you are. It will also aid and supplement the manifesting process, as it keeps you in that upbeat frame of mind.

You can start your affirmations at this very moment. Think of a positive statement right now about who you are and repeat it three times, either aloud or in your head.

You may think that repeating a statement to yourself can't possibly do anything to boost confidence; however, there is a bit of science behind this accepted form of talking to yourself. A statement, whether positive or negative, if repeated enough over time, eventually trickles down into the subconscious, and so the statement becomes a reality for you. By replacing any negative thoughts with positive ones, all those happy and sunny vibes will start to do wonders for your sense of self.

The beauty of affirmations is that you can continually experiment with them to suit how you feel at any given moment. To start with, you may want to practise a general life-affirming statement:

I am a fabulous person

It may seem a little strange at first repeating 'I am a fabulous person' and yet, when you think about it, it isn't really that unusual. If we don't accept and embrace all that is great about ourselves, why would anyone else?

I would suggest setting aside a very speedy minute per day to give the affirmation your undivided focus and energy. The way to really empower the affirmation is to say it in front of a mirror and aloud. If you prefer, you can also sing the affirmation, or yell it with all your goddess might.

Examples of affirmations

◆ I am seizing every opportunity that comes my way.
◆ I am positive and excited about my day.
◆ I am a lovely person.

Always keep your affirmations in the present, so rather than saying, 'I am going to achieve my goal of . . .' replace it with 'I am achieving my goal of . . .'

And remember, you can change the affirmation if you feel your current one isn't working for you. The affirmation should always feel right for you.

Spiritual Goddess tip

Have an affirmation in mind before that important first date. For extra 'pow' repeat the affirmation in front of a mirror.

Manifesting a new BFF (only fabulous people need apply!)

We can all count ourselves lucky if we have found that true friendship – the kind of relationship where you just 'fit together' in your own unique and wonderful way. A friendship is something to be cherished, and you know when you have found that special friend for life. By comparison, you also know when you have attracted the 'wrong' kind of friend – the one you look back on and wonder, *What on earth was I thinking?*

If you feel at this moment that you are lacking in the 'true' kind of friendship, and feel your circle could do with a bit of a makeover, why not take the opportunity to manifest a new gal pal. Why settle for a so-so friendship?

Try creating a friend checklist, and add to your 'ultimate wish list'. My list is below, for your amusement:

◆ Crazy sense of humour – laughter is essential.

◆ Someone I can share my secrets with, without feeling they will appear on Facebook 30 minutes later – a big no-no.

◆ A friend who has a shared love of the arts – theatre, music, comedy, and the odd trip to a gallery where we proceed to spend most of our time in the gift shop (always more fun).

◆ Someone who likes good conversation, with a splash of girly gossip for good measure.

◆ A person who has a genuinely good heart and wants the best for me (no energy-zappers allowed).

Tailor your list to your specific 'wants', but also keep open-minded. Our new friend will never be the cookie-cutter image of perfection, and yet we wouldn't want them to be. It's all those weird and wonderful little eccentricities that makes her the friend we love and cherish. So start to create those opportunities now to help meet new friends: say 'yes' to any invitation that comes your way; make an effort to speak to that person who always looks so friendly and who you've wanted to speak to for ages; and join that group which you have secretly wanted to but have been hesitant to do so. Absolutely nothing can be lost from simply having a go. You've asked the universe for what you want, now work towards making it happen. Manifest away, ladies, and snag that BFF.

Spiritual Goddess tip

As you start to manifest more regularly you will find opportunities will present themselves a lot quicker as you 'attune' to the universe. Basically, the more you practise, the better at manifesting you will become.

Exercise
Make a dream board

Have scissors, glue and felt tip pens at the ready. For this exercise, you can rewind the years to a much simpler time when a pair of scissors, a glue stick, and a box of glitter was the most exciting part of your day. It can be therapeutic to create, as it allows us to feel and see what we are aiming for. Cutting and sticking is not just for kids.

Creating a 'dream board' is a tangible reminder of everything you wish to accomplish. All you need is a large sheet of paper, A3 or bigger. If you happen to have a cork board currently on your wall, even better.

1. Your board/sheet of paper will act as your visual prompt, which will include: cuttings, photos, writings – all the things you want to accomplish and wish to improve upon; for example, you may decide that working on your relationships is most important to you right now. If you and a friend are going through something of a 'drought' and everything feels a bit stale, pin a photo on your board of a particularly happy moment between the two of you, and it will remind you of where your energy needs to be focused.

2. The career-orientated goddess may choose to fill her board with inspirational ideas focused around a career goal. If, for example, your ambition is to enter the world of fashion, fill your board with clippings, photos, colour swatches – anything you can find that

involves the world in which you want to work. The clippings should be emotive, and give you the impetus to want to pursue that goal.

3. If your dream is to go travelling, trawl those travel brochures and find cut-outs of landmarks of your chosen destination. If your dream is to visit Paris, find a cut-out of a famous Parisian landmark to pin on your board.

4. The board can also contain your own musings and thoughts, and any quotes or pieces of literature which have sparked your creative thinking. Above all, you should feel motivated when you look at your dream board.

5. You can also use your board to bolster your love life. If you are ready for a spot of romance, you can make a list of the attributes you are looking for, and then add them to your board. As an additional 'love supplement', pin a piece of jewellery containing rose quartz (the 'love' crystal) to keep those heart-shaped vibes coming your way.

The board doesn't have to be in any particular order. The pictures can be wherever you want them to be, or where your instinct takes you. Just ensure all of the clippings are visible. And, of course, like everything in life, our dreams often change, so as soon as you have fulfilled an ambition, or if you change your mind on a particular 'want', simply remove the picture and replace it with one of your new goals.

Spend as much time as possible observing your board, so keep it in a place where it's easy to view. Look over your dream clippings, and allow yourself to visualise achieving your aim.

The dream board is a manifestation of everything you want your life to be, so if there's anything that you desire, pin it on that board. The great thing is, it will bring to focus all that you want to accomplish, and the more you set out to achieve, the more dreams will be born as a result.

Spiritual Goddess tip

Enjoy nurturing your dreams, and keep them alive with daily reinforcements. Why not visualise just before you go to sleep or while taking a bath? What could be better than chilling out and feeling inspired all at the same time?

Your wish is at **your** command

In that eternal quest to make our most desired of wishes come true, it inevitably falls to that one person to make it all happen: you. At times, you may wish you had your very own 'dream team' working alongside you 24/7 to help turn that dream into a reality; however, the immense satisfaction you'll feel when you make it happen for yourself is a far more exciting prospect.

It may sound a little clichéd, but there is absolutely nothing and no one who can stand in your way once your mind is set on achieving a goal. That doesn't mean to say you won't come up against obstacles, believe me. Start stretching those calf muscles, ladies, as there will doubtless be a few curve balls thrown your way to deter you from your course, and the faster you can react and adapt to the situation, the quicker you will get back on track.

Persistence has an incredible way of breaking down barriers that you might not have thought possible and, over time, your continued efforts will pay off, and there is nothing more satisfying than achieving that end result. If you feel a little universal assistance would be of help, going through the process of manifesting can bring that much needed focus and clarity to your goals.

I think it's about time we did away with the proverbial magic wand, and boxed up those old ruby slippers. The 21st-century goddess is in the business of making the magic happen herself.

Where, Oh Where, is My One True Love! Aka the Soul Mate

I wonder if you have ever used the phrase, 'I think he/she is my soul mate' or 'I love him with all my heart and soul'? Sound familiar? I think we can all agree that we have used the soul many a time in expressing our deepest desire for a guy . . . or indeed that gorgeous bracelet you've had your eye on for some time.

We also use the word soul when we feel someone is lacking in empathy for another person, and on those occasions we may feel that person is 'soulless'. And yet, none of us is born without one; in fact, it would be quite impossible to function without a soul.

You may be wondering what this soul is that we speak so passionately about? To answer that question: your soul is that unique spark, or indefinable 'thing' that makes you the extra-ordinary person you are. The soul gives our human body 'life', and without it, we would be nothing more than an empty shell.

The purpose of the soul is to experience all that life has to offer, and there is certainly a huge selection on the menu: love, friendship, joy, and hope, even the bitter taste of disappointment. It is said that our more difficult times are there to help us grow, and that is very true. It is often in the more testing moments that we become stronger in character and more resilient because of it.

Your soul makes a decision on what it hopes to achieve in every incarnation, otherwise known as a lifetime. The soul is like the perpetual student, hungry for knowledge and is always eager to learn and experience more.

Each soul has its very own personalised blueprint of what it hopes to achieve and experience in a lifetime. If these experiences are not fully achieved, the soul may wish to experience them in another incarnation. When you feel excited or passionate about a career choice, a relationship, or simply a deep connection to your life choices, it is a sign that you are travelling along the path that is right for you.

The soul is working towards achieving a vast knowledge of human experience. It then becomes interesting to realise that we all have our unique paths in life, and comparing ourselves to others becomes a completely futile exercise. Although we may have similar views, ideas and common interests as friends and family, we are all unique on a soul level.

Reincarnation

It is said that it can take a lifetime to learn the soul lessons, but have you ever considered that you may already have spent many lifetimes in the classroom of life?

Reincarnation is the belief that our soul incarnates again and again (and again) on the earth plane in order to experience as much of life as is humanly and spiritually possible.

You may be thinking to yourself, *If I have so many past lives, why can't I remember them?* The likelihood is that you do remember, but in a far more fragmented way. It's a bit like the pieces of a jigsaw: you join them together step by step. You may, for example, have an irrational fear which you have never fully understood. It could well be that the fear is connected with a past life experience that caused much anxiety for you, and so you are being presented with the same issue in this life until that fear has been finally conquered. Once we have learned the lesson and faced that fear, we will be presented with a new life lesson.

Another indication that a past experience may be seeping into your present is the feeling of 'knowing' very detailed, specific information about a town, city or even a country without ever having visited before. It may feel like an instant connection, as if it was a place you knew very well – it could well be a location where you had lived in a previous life.

Spiritual Goddess tip

How to look out for possible previous life experiences:

- Feelings of familiarity when you visit a town or city you haven't been to before.
- An instant rapport with someone you have only just met – you may have had a relationship with their incarnated self in a past life.
- You know very detailed information about a person, place or object of which you have no rational explanation.

Keep an open mind when piecing together the puzzle of a past-life experience: listen to what your intuition is telling you, and if you want to delve even further, ask your angels to wing a few clues your way – pun intended!

Reincarnation

The belief that we live and experience many lifetimes,
not just the one right now.

Learning the soul lessons

The soul is rather like the student who always sits at the front of
the class, is never late, and soaks up every last drop of information like a sponge, whereas the rest of the class is just hanging on
for the sweet relief of home time.

It's good to know that our soul lessons are not confined to the
four walls of a classroom but are experienced through our daily
interaction with people. Learning our unique soul lessons can
be achieved quite easily by simply taking stock of your life right
now, and considering those areas that you feel could do with a
little TLC. I say 'unique' soul lessons as every one of us has a
completely different set of lessons to learn from and experience.

To begin, think about an aspect of your life which you find
difficult to deal with. You may, for example, be really outgoing
within your social group, and yet the idea of speaking
aloud in a public forum may have you quaking in
your high-heeled boots. It's interesting how we
tend to shy away from those areas in which
we feel most unsure or less confident about,
and yet it is these areas where we often learn
our most valuable soul lessons.

How to spot a soul lesson

◆ You feel nervous about confronting a particular issue in your life.
◆ You shy away from specific subjects, or change the conversation because you feel unsure of yourself.
◆ You don't speak up for fear you are not good enough.

We all have a 'thing', as I like to call it, which we would prefer not to deal with, and yet the universe will keep presenting us with the same issue in order that we learn from it. The upside to facing a fear is that once it has been faced, the lesson is learned and it is no longer that tiresome problem that took up so much of your time and energy. It then allows more time to focus on the enjoyable things in life.

What is a soul mate?

When you meet a soul mate for the very first time, it is a feeling like no other: it's as if you have known the person for your entire life. The reason you feel that immediate connection when you meet a soul mate is that your relationship may have spanned many lifetimes, and so it is, quite literally, like meeting an old friend. With a soul mate, you usually find that you have much to talk about, and the relationship between the two of you may seem very natural.

You have many different kinds of soul mates, not all of them romantic. The stereotype for a soul mate is that you have to fall madly in love with them at first sight, which is simply not the case. The majority of your soul mates will be the friends and family who surround you in your life right now. Of course, when you do meet that romantic soul mate it can be an awesomely powerful experience, so brace yourself for the head-over-heels scenario that will surely ensue.

Twin flame: the 'love' mate

Where the soul mate ends, the 'twin flame' surely begins. Take a deep breath, as I'm about to introduce you to a soul mate of the type which is bound to stoke the flames of passion. Your twin flame is your 'true' soul mate, that other half which cannot be replicated, as that person is, quite literally, your other half. And when you meet that person it is like finding that missing piece of the love puzzle – it's the perfect fit for you.

Spiritually speaking, your twin flame is notoriously hard to find, as both flames seek to evolve and learn as much as possible in order to create that perfect union together. Twin flames generally meet when they are both at a point in their lives when they are ready to work together as a team – it really is a true meeting of minds. In turn, it makes them that much harder to find, as you are both so busy learning and nurturing your own spirit that finding the right moment can be tricky. When you do (finally!) meet, boy, do the sparks fly! The relationship between twin flames can be a very passionate and intense experience.

You may be wondering what you are expected to feel when you meet this flickering flame of desire. It would, of course, be ideal if a special 'twin flame alarm' sounded off the moment you hit the love jackpot; however, you have to rely on your own alarm bell, aka your intuition, to decipher whether you have indeed met your true match. It is also said that once you meet your twin flame you will find it incredibly hard to be apart from them, as the connection between the two of you is so strong, not only in a physical sense but also on a psychic level. You may find there is a telepathic connection, and you both share a strong sense of what the other is thinking, feeling, or about to say. It is a connection that really does tick every box – compatible in every department.

Just one word of twin flame caution: keep open-minded and don't dismiss the fabulous guys out there who are looking for 'you' right now. Twin flames don't always meet in the same incarnation, remember; it's a bit like arranging a date, and sometimes the lines of communication can get a little muddled: you've been waiting an hour, but he's running two behind. So don't hang around, say 'yes' to that other great guy, and who knows, he may spark the flames of passion too.

Karma: good girl versus bad girl

Think back to your early years at school, otherwise known as the time when you spent most of your day finger-painting – that far back. Do you recall the reward system in place for all your good behaviour? Perhaps you were awarded those coveted gold stars, or maybe you were given an extra blue tick against your workbook. Whatever the reward system, didn't we all feel that wave of achievement for those good deeds? However, for all the gold-star goodness, there was also another system in place for our 'not so good' behaviour, and for those offences, it often resulted in being sent to the back of the class to stare at the wall for the remainder of the lesson or, horror of horrors, the teacher retracting that hard-earned gold star from the wall chart.

I think the universal system of reward for good deeds versus punishment for the unmentionable, perfectly captures the concept of karma – the universal law of 'what goes around, comes around'. Everything we choose to do or say has a consequence attached to it. It can sound a little scary, but I promise it's not.

Over the course of our lifetime we accrue karma, whether it be the gold-star good stuff, or the plain old rubbishy not-worth-thinking-about stuff. I think we can all relate to the feeling when our karmic sheet of good deeds and not-so-good deeds are running a close 50:50 tie. Karma can indeed have the modern goddess all of a stress – I know how difficult it can be to do and say the right thing all of the time. To put your minds at rest from our karmic record, remember this: nobody's perfect, and we all make mistakes. The mischievous goddess within us is capable of being unleashed at any time – don't we all wish that the person who just shoulder-barged us in the street would fall down with a great 'thwack!'? It's naughty, but true.

How can the modern goddess not get a little ruffled from time to time with so much going on in a day? Say, for example, you haven't been feeling your usual shiny self, and you recognise you have been a little mad at the world. The best way to achieve a few cosmic brownie points is to focus on keeping your thoughts and actions as positive as possible – why not increase your daily affirmations and repeat aloud for an extra boost? And just before you leave your home in the morning, mentally surround yourself with your protective bubble to keep those negative nasties at bay.

If we never put a foot wrong, we wouldn't learn much at all so, as much as I personally adhere to the guidelines of karma, I whole-heartedly believe that mistakes are allowed – in fact, they're vital to our soul's growth.

The life lessons we are experiencing now may also be a result of our karmic record, and in order to work out our karma, the most positive action we can take is to embrace what challenges life throws at us; for example, next time you feel a little angry at the world, take a moment to think about what it is that is actually bothering you. If you can start to glean the root of the problem, you can start to take those steps to tackling the issue.

A word of advice on karma: never guilt trip yourself into trying to live your life like the perfect saint or angel. It's their job to achieve such perfection! The modern goddess is a far-off but promising second. Oh, to earn a set of wings. Our task is to live the best life we can by spreading as much positive energy as a modern goddess can. Now, I think that deserves an extra gold star, don't you?

Karma

The law of 'cause and effect', otherwise known as 'what goes around, comes around'. We're all working towards achieving a good karmic record, so the more cosmic brownie points the better.

Your soul group, aka the leading players!

I think there are far too many amazing people in this world to have just the 'one' soul mate. I like the idea of having one or two, maybe even three or four – the more the merrier in fact. As I mentioned earlier in the chapter, a soul mate isn't exclusively a romantic partner; in fact, did you know that your best friend is a soul mate? OK, so you may not get butterflies when you see her, but that person is a part of your bigger soul group.

I see the soul group like the cast of a great film. Think of your favourite film, preferably one with a big ensemble cast, and now put yourself in the starring role of leading lady and then cast your family and friends in the other roles. The new love, or indeed potential love interest, can be cast as the new leading man. Your friends and family will be in the supporting roles, while the people you encounter day in, day out, will be the recurring, walk-on roles.

Your soul group is your very own cast of players, and you have all chosen to work together in order to learn your unique soul lessons. Of course, like any ensemble cast, the roles change, and so the leading man in your life right now may take on a lesser role next time around, depending on what lessons are needed to be learned. The beauty of the soul group is that every person has an important part to play, no matter how big or small.

It's also important to know that a soul mate doesn't have to agree with everything you say or do; in fact, some of our most important soul mates are the ones that challenge and encourage us to deal with our issues head-on.

As the leading lady of your soul group, remember that no cast will ever be perfect, you will encounter leading lady/leading man disagreements, a supporting player may want their part bumped to a leading role, and some of your walk-on cast may disappear altogether – and that's OK too. You'll have your moments where life is going great, and you're interacting well with friends and family. In turn, you will also have your moments where you find yourself bickering with your boyfriend (leading man), perhaps losing touch with your best friend (lead supporting role) and it seems the whole show and everyone in it is falling apart. Just know that it will all come together again as soon as you start working as a team.

Doesn't it shine a whole new light on the definition of 'soul mates'?

Soul group

The souls you have chosen to work with and learn from through your various incarnations on the earth plane.

The love that wasn't forever

When a relationship comes to an end, there is a tendency to wash our hands of all evidence that there was even a relationship to begin with. Hands up who has hastily scrapped all photos/text messages/cuddly toys in a fit of post-break-up despair? We suddenly become the criminal mastermind in the art of disposing of all traces of the relationship, subsequently reducing ourselves to an obsessive repetition of 'What went wrong?', excess chocolate consumption, and taking up permanent residence on the couch. A love that wasn't forever is, indeed, a tough pill to swallow.

Not all 'love' is there for the long haul. Some romances are short, exciting thrill rides that leave you breathless but eventually run out of steam.

Relationships often just run their course, but that doesn't make them any less important. Try to think about it this way: did he make you laugh, put a smile on your face when you were feeling blue, encourage you to better yourself and pursue what you wanted to do? If you answered 'yes' to at least one of these questions, you can be sure it was a relationship worth having. And whoever made up the rule that a relationship has to last forever? If the relationship has taught you something, then that person has been as much a soul mate as the one who stays with you for a lifetime.

Confrontational souls: is there any spell to 'magic' them away?

Not all soul mates will make our heart skip a beat, in fact, many of our soul mates leave a lot to be desired. It does make you wonder if you could somehow conjure up a witchy brew to miraculously rid the more troublesome soul mates from your life with a vanishing spell.

It is a common ground that we all experience: the difficulties of human relationships. We all have to deal with those individuals who we would rather walk three extra streets not to have to face, let alone have a conversation with. It may surprise you to know that these tricky individuals play an important role in our lives, and can act as our soul teachers.

Soul teachers are those individuals who have something to teach us about the person we are and, often, the person we are to become.

From reading this, you may have already thought of one or two characters who you find difficult to deal with. You may be thinking that if you are in charge of your own show, why would you invite confrontational, difficult people into your life? It may comfort you to know that these individuals are perhaps some of the most significant characters of all. At times, I dare say, they are of equal importance as your lead players. You may, for example, have a friend or family member who you find extremely problematic and, try as you may, you just can't see eye to eye on any issue. Their difficult nature may shine a light on what it is you are finding difficult to deal with or are choosing to ignore. If it is the case that this person seems critical of you and your choices – say, for example, you have your heart set on a particular career path and for some reason they seem to be doing their level best to deter you from your course – why not ask yourself why you let their comments affect you? If you sit down and really think about it, why would you care what this person thinks, who is clearly being of no support to you whatsoever? Their issue is more tellingly about their own shortcomings and lack of self-esteem.

Spiritual Goddess tip

Surround yourself with your protective bubble when dealing with difficult, energy-zapping situations.

It is often when we are placed in tricky situations that we learn the most about ourselves. Here are a few tips I have found helpful myself when dealing with these tricky teachers:

◆ Find a quiet time to take the person aside and mention the concern you have. A loud argument in the middle of a shopping centre is never conducive to a happy relationship. A quiet moment between the two of you might help clear the air.

◆ Writing a letter can be a therapeutic way of releasing any anger or upset you feel, and can also act as a gentle yet effective way of expressing what it is that is bothering you. In conversation, we sometimes forget what it is we want to say (I know I do), whereas a letter can put across your most personal feelings which can sometimes be hard to articulate in conversation.

◆ Think about what you want out of the relationship, and, more importantly, what you don't. You deserve to be surrounded by people who care and want the very best for you.

If you have taken the step to confront the issue, you have played your part, and in doing so, have dealt with that fear – well done you.

How to find your soul mate (the romantic one that is)

When you have been hit by cupid's heart-shaped arrow you'll recognise that special, one-of-a-kind feeling. The moment could be straight from a scene of your favourite romantic movie – you know, the part where their eyes meet across a crowded room, and for that brief moment, time seems to stand still. In real life, the moment plays more along the lines of: eyes meet across a crowded shop floor; your heart skips a beat, transfixed by 'the one'; you move forward for closer inspection – *Is it really them?* you wonder; as you lovingly look into the bejewelled eye of the diamanté embellishment adorning those black satin strappy heels, it is then you realise there is such a thing as sole mates. Oh, the romance of it all.

Finding the perfect shoes that match every outfit, the handbag that fits all, or the day dress that can double up as evening wear are those rare finds you discover once in a blue moon – the kind of items you can't put a price on. At least, we choose not to acknowledge those pesky little tags with the frustratingly large digits.

The same could be said for love, that elusive find you can't really put a price on. You can also guarantee that when you're ready for a little romance in your life, there seems to be an underwhelming shortage of stock. You survey your current choices, and it seems as though you've been presented with a load of old hand-me-downs. The guy who has been asking you out for some time, for example, starts to look like an appealing option.

From the moment we read our first fairytale we have become hooked on the idea of the elusive 'knight in shining armour', who whisks us off our feet and proceeds to ride us off into the sunset. In reality, we are more likely to be thrown off the horse when the 'knight' suddenly realises he's double-booked, and we're stuck with taking the bus home.

Our ever-resilient hearts are willing to try, try, and indeed, try again when it comes to love. Why is it when we fall over and hurt ourselves we are so careful not to fall again, and yet, when it comes to love, we are more than willing to fall head over heels again and again, sustaining all manner of heart-related injuries?

It begs the question: what is it about the elusive soul mate that has the power to send even the most level-headed goddess all of a flutter? And why is it that we are looking for this one special mate, when it's probably more realistic to embrace the one right now.

Searching for that soul mate – the one that hits like a *coup de foudre*, or love at first sight – is the most coveted of all the soul mates, because when all is said and done, we simply want to feel that extra-special connection with another person.

As is the nature of relationships, the moment you stop looking for one is the moment you find it. But there is no harm in working your feminine magic to bring about those love vibes asap.

Step 1: the dream guy

Do you have pen and paper handy, ladies? OK, let's begin. The mysterious nature of love can happen at any time, anywhere, and when we least expect it, and frustratingly, it usually does. And yet, if we are unclear ourselves as to what it is we really want, it makes it that much harder to spot when a great opportunity is right in front of us. Imagine: the most amazing guy has come into your life and, because of your hesitation, the opportunity passes you by. If we can be clear in our minds as to our ideal relationship, then there is every chance that you will snag that perfect catch.

Exercise
Imagine the dream guy

1. Jot down the kind of relationship you're after. At this point it's tempting to note down the dream vital stats: tall, dark, handsome – any of these sound familiar? But as is the nature of love, the person you fall for will rarely look like the image you have created in your mind. You may have a type that you usually go for, but when that perfect guy comes your way, any 'type' should go flying out of the window – you wouldn't let a good man slip through your fingers because of contrary hair colour, after all.
2. Be as open as you can with this list, as we are looking specifically at personality traits; for example:
   • Outdoorsy
   • Sensitive and caring
   • Likes hanging out in a big social group
   • Enjoys nights in just as much as nights out
   • Has goals for himself, and is passionate about what he wants to do with his life

---

This handy little love list will work alongside the next step in finding that romantic mate.

Step 2: what do I want in a relationship?

Take time out to start actively visualising your ideal relationship. Put into practice the manifesting principles outlined earlier in the book (see Chapter 5).

Exercise
Picture your relationship

1. Create a picture in your mind of what you want from a new relationship, and give it what I like to call the 'reality makeover', meaning, keep the visual in a reality you are familiar with. If, for example, a walk through the local park and grabbing a coffee sounds like a plausible first-date scenario for you, keep the visual along this kind of framework. Visualising your first date on a yacht in the Caribbean is probably not the norm for most people, so remember to keep the visual real to you.

2. By all means keep the visual fun and creative, and dream as vividly as you want, but as this is an active visual with the 'intent' of manifesting a potential boyfriend, you want to ensure it is authentic to your personal experience.

3. Once that visual is clear, and you feel it is a real possibility, keep reliving the scenarios in your mind, and take time to give 'life' to the visual every day. Imagine going on dates, spending time at your place, introducing him to your friends. It is when we become clear in our minds as to what we want that the universe receives those crystal-clear messages too.

Step 3: guardian angel to the rescue

What would we do without our guardian angel? From career choices, family issues, to matters of the beating heart, your Guardian Angel is your most trusted of your ethereal entourage! To that end, your Guardian Angel can be a very helpful ally when looking for a romantic soul mate.

Exercise
Contact your Guardian Angel

1. At a time that is right for you, contact your Guardian Angel and describe the kind of love you are looking for, and explain what you hope for this potential new boyfriend.
2. I would suggest speaking aloud, as it reaffirms your request.

Step 4: affirmative action

There is nothing more powerful than a proactive goddess when on the hunt for a new heart's desire.

Take a 360-degree look at your social life. Is there a special someone who you've reduced to no more than a walk-on part, and haven't seriously considered getting to know better? Many of us adhere to the notion that if we are not immediately struck with the arrow of desire then that person is not worth a second glance. I think we need to toss away those outdated ideas that love strikes us like a thunderbolt. I certainly don't disagree with the idea, and 'thunderbolt' love can happen, but I also think there are probably more than a few hidden gems in your life right now. Sure, they may need a little polishing up, but once you see them cast in a new light (the pink hue of love) you may realise that there is more to that person than you initially thought. If you feel even the smallest inkling that the guy who has been a recurring player in your life may have the 'luuurve' factor, consider boosting him to supporting-role status, and who knows, one day he may even be promoted to 'leading man'.

Angelic tips

Guidance from angels and spirit guides comes through in those wee small hours when we're in the midst of dreaming about that 'dream' guy. Keep alert for any symbolism, and use your intuition to decipher what it means to you. Our dreams offer those all-important cryptic clues that require our innate detective skills. Text a friend and ask her opinion on the matter and those symbolic messages will be revealed in no time.

Do you know that your Guardian Angel can communicate with the angel of your soul mate? If you want to really get your Guardian Angel working for you, I suggest asking them to make contact with the angels of your romantic soul mate, so that they can start to cosmically move the process along.

Our guardian angel can provide us with emotional and spiritual help, and yet if we refuse to take decisive action for ourselves, we will never bag that leading man. So, put down that popcorn, grab a friend, sister or cousin – whoever is up for doing something different – and spend a few hours out of the comfort of the sofa, in the knowledge that you may meet that potential 'someone'.

If you see a poster for an evening class for dance or theatre, take the initiative and join in. It doesn't matter if you've never had a burning desire to learn the tango, or the fact that 'treading the boards' has never featured on your 'to do' list, joining a class or group can be a lot of fun, and an inventive way of meeting new people you might not have ordinarily socialised with.

Step 5: love will come, ladies, so just relax and enjoy yourself

Are you constantly looking at the proverbial love clock? Counting down the minutes until 'he' arrives? Most of us suffer from a chronic lack of patience – I know I do – and it can feel like you have been waiting 'for ever' for the perfect guy to come along. The feeling of wanting that special someone in your life conflicts with the reality that sometimes we all have to be a little more patient. Rarely does true love turn up at the door at the precise time and day which suits us best – if love was as convenient as next-day delivery, we would, of course, all be waiting by the door.

As soon as you put him out of your mind is the moment when he arrives.

So many 'souls', so little time

As soon as you see the bigger 'soul picture' you will realise how important all the people in your life really are. We all have our favourite souls who we adore spending time with and hope will stick around for the duration of our show, and then there are those who we find a little more difficult to deal with, and yet they also have a part to play. And when it comes to the idea of the 'one' true soul mate, it is a choice that can only ever be made by you. No one can tell you when you have met the 'right' one.

My one little piece of advice is to consider the person you are right now, and then to visualise how much you are set to experience over a lifetime. The likelihood is that you will attract all different types of soul mates depending on your mood, state of mind, and who happens to catch your eye. It is all a choice, so enjoy the experience – 'love', as they say, is a feeling like no other.

And remember, always keep in mind all the fabulous people out there just waiting to meet a like-minded soul like you.

Soul mate

A person you have known and encountered over many lifetimes. You will feel an instant connection with a soul mate.

Spiritually Cleanse
Your Home

Can you recall the scariest ghost story you were ever told? I remember one particular tale so terrifying it had my friends and I cowering beneath the covers. The sleepless night was made all the more amusing when we had to escort each other to the bathroom for fear we would be picked off one by one.

For you ladies out there who love a good ghost story or two – and I'm one of them – I feel obliged to inform you that the following chapter may dispel a few of the old myths relating to those ghostly tales from childhood. In the bright light of day, the ghosts of our nightmares are a far more straight-forward paranormal happening, and are simply part of the greater spiritual spectrum.

In our younger years, we did not always apply such logical thinking to all things that went bump in the night. Our home became a battleground between 'us' and 'them', aka the ghostly creatures that lurked under our bed at night. We couldn't be blamed for thinking this; after all, the grisly stories depicted on film always seemed to be centred around the family home – not great news when you hear the drip, drip, dripping sound in the bathroom late at night.

The modern goddess can learn to uncover the truth behind these spine-tingling tales, and reclaim her bedroom from the energy-draining, happy-zapping vibes, transforming it into a space of peace, tranquillity and, most importantly, 'ghost' free.

Things that go bump in the night

I once visited a stately home where there was rumoured to be a haunting. As a youngster, I was, of course, fascinated to discover this, and it was the only reason I was so eager to visit in the first place. Having had an experience of seeing what I now know as spirit, I was curious to see another person of what I used to call the 'invisible kind'. I looked closely for any ghostly images in the mirror, sounds of frantic footsteps, or even mournful sobbing but, in fact, the only sobbing audible was from a small child nearby who was clearly as unimpressed as I was. I came to the conclusion that real-life hauntings were not as reliable as those in film.

The 'hauntings' depicted on film in any case are usually assigned to those eerie Gothic mansions, with thunderstorms and scary-looking butlers. A haunting – to take away the grisly myth attached to it – occurs when a psychic imprint is left behind in a home, building, or even a street. This energetic imprint keeps replaying over and over again, and is called a 'residual haunting'. The haunting may involve:

◆ Repeated rapping on doors or walls
◆ Moaning

◆ Wailing

◆ The sound of footsteps running up and down corridors

There is a repetitive rhythm to this type of haunting, and the activity often takes place at specific times during the day or night. A haunting of this kind occurs when something particularly distressing has taken place, which is the reason for the powerful psychic imprint that remains. The building has literally taken on the energy of that past event, even though it may have happened years, even hundreds of years, previously.

The other kind of haunting is the one we are all very familiar with, and it is of the more ghostly variety. The superstar of the supernatural has always been the ghost. I think most of us will agree that our first understanding of anything to do with the mysterious 'other realm' or the 'spiritual' has to be the image of the white sheet flying around of its own accord in typically ghostly fashion. The ghost has subsequently been typecast in this terrifying role.

It's also interesting why the idea of a ghost has always instilled such fear and discontent. Could it be that we all assume ghosts are there to spook us out? Or, perhaps it is because we don't really encounter them on a regular basis and so it is far removed from our reality. If we all had a friendly ghost that roamed as freely as the family cat, we would view it as the norm, and not an extraordinary event. And yet, these mysterious wanderers of the night have a far more down-to-earth explanation.

A ghostly presence occurs when a soul hasn't moved on after experiencing physical death. The soul may not have realised that they should be passing to the next realm, or perhaps feels confused and frightened to do so, and so remains in a kind of limbo state, whereby they repeat the same actions and series of movements over and over again as when alive. The ghost may, at times, try to interact with the living, and can be easily sussed out if you suspect the following:

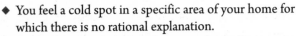

How to recognise a ghostly presence

♦ You feel a cold spot in a specific area of your home for which there is no rational explanation.
♦ Repetitive sounds of running up or down the stairs/tapping/banging on walls.
♦ You suddenly smell a strong odour or scent, as if someone had just entered the room.
♦ You feel a presence around you through which you feel unease or discomfort. It may leave you feeling tired or sad.

Have you seen a ghost?

It's the burning question on everyone's lips from the moment we watched our first scary movie, to the time we shared ghost stories deep into the night. We all wanted to know who had actually seen a ghost. The sight of such paranormal phenomena is in fact most commonly associated with young people, particularly in childhood and through to the early teenage years. It may prompt you to think back to your own formative experiences.

Children are more likely to pick up on ghostly activity than adults, as they have an open, non-judgemental view of life and are far more aware and in tune with their psychic self.

If you think back to your childhood, you may have seen a ghostly presence and did not realise it at the time. Ask yourself some questions to see if you can shed any light on any early psychic experiences:

- Could I feel a presence around me that could not be rationally explained?
- Did I ever catch sight of a person in my home who could not have been a family member and wasn't somebody I knew was visiting?
- Can I remember having an imaginary friend who I could see as clearly as my real ones?

You may find that you did tune into the psychic world a lot more than you realised. Also, the happenings may not have been specifically a 'ghost', but could have well been a spirit guide who was with you.

If you currently feel that you have come upon a presence either in your own home, or a friend has mentioned she feels unusual activity at her place, there are steps you can take to help clear your home of any uninvited visitors.

Before you begin

Just before you start, make sure you consider all household possibilities. I know the feeling when you're home alone and you suddenly hear the sound of knocking, dripping or even footsteps. It's enough to have you reaching for your door key. In actual fact, suspected ghostly happenings are often the bumps, thumps and rumblings of the house itself. The footsteps you can hear above may in fact be those of your next-door neighbour padding about their bedroom. The moans and sobs coming from the living-room wall could well be the grief-stricken next-door neighbour who just found out his team lost the match.

Once you have checked, and double-checked all household possibilities, you can then move on to the next step.

Exercise
'Bye-bye ghostie'

To rid your house of the suspected ghostly presence, there are steps you can take to set your temporary visitor on his journey home. The steps are simple, easy to carry out, and even better if you can do them with a friend. The ideal location to carry out the exercise is in the room where you feel the presence is most strong.

Before you begin, always remember to surround yourself with your protective bubble (page 29), ground (page 30), and ask that your Guardian Angel remain close.

1. Light an incense stick, preferably one that is especially cleansing and purifying, such as sage or frankincense. Place the incense in the holder on a secure ledge, and open all doors in the home to ensure every room is infused with the cleansing aroma. You can task your friend with this step.

2. This next step involves letting the ghost know that they do not belong in your home, and ask that they leave immediately. For this, it is advisable to speak aloud and keep a firm and confident tone. You may also want to inform them of the current time and date, so that they are aware of the reality of their situation – something they themselves have never faced.

3. Call upon the angels around you to help the trapped spirit to move on. The angels have the power to help make the transition to the next step on their journey. You can call upon angelic assistance either aloud or in your mind. Ask in the way that is comfortable and real for you.

4. Once you have asked the angels to help, surround yourself again with the white, purifying light. This time, also make sure that you surround your home with the light. To do this, simply close your eyes and visualise your home, and then see it being surrounded and filled with positive and purifying light. And then the final step is to 'ground' yourself.

Once you have come to the end of step 4, remember to extinguish the incense stick carefully. You may want to wander about your home and get a sense of any change in atmosphere. Does it feel different? Has the cold spot gone from the room? You can also note down the experience and the changes you feel have occurred. To keep the energy around you balanced and positive, you can start to apply 'cleansing' rituals to your home regularly, so keep reading for the space-clearing exercise coming up.

Ghost

A soul who has not moved on after physical death, caught between two worlds, is commonly termed a 'ghost'.

Poltergeists (no throwing my favourite shoes!)

I remember when I first heard about poltergeists – the most mischievous of the paranormal phenomena – and recoiled in horror when I found out their 'signature' calling card.

As you may have read about or even seen on TV, the most common characteristic of the poltergeist involves items from the home suddenly being thrown at random. At the time, I was something of a neat-freak (oh, how times have changed) and the thought of my neatly arranged books suddenly being hurled by a phantom was not an ideal situation.

The word 'poltergeist' translates from the German word meaning 'rumbling ghost'. The manifestation generally occurs as a result of a member of the household experiencing some kind of emotional trauma or distress. This person may not give away any visual clues of their emotional problems; instead, it is said their intense feelings of anger or rage can set off and activate the disruptive poltergeist activity, causing much mayhem for the unsuspecting inhabitants of that home.

Examples of poltergeist activity

◆ Objects being thrown across the room
◆ Lights flickering on and off
◆ Furniture/household objects moving
◆ Banging/thumping sounds on the wall

This most unwelcome of paranormal happenings is highly unlikely to be the cause of your house rumblings and grumblings. In fact, the most probable cause of items being thrown across the room are those pair of old shoes you just found at the bottom of your wardrobe, leading to the horrifying item being flung across the room in typically dramatic fashion.

Poltergeist

A manifestation that causes mayhem and chaos through their mischievous actions. The happenings are said to be a result of an unconscious build-up of emotion in one of the occupants of the home.

Your psychic pet

Animals are highly psychic and intuitive, and are able to pick up on the invisible world around them. Cats in particular are attuned with their psychic sense. You may have already noticed when they have picked up on something and sit transfixed by an otherwise blank space in the room.

If you notice that your pet has started a pattern of behaviour such as entering a particular room and staring at a spot on the wall, or an empty space, you may want to try the 'space clearing' exercise coming up. Animals not only pick up on ghostly activity but also the energetic activity in a room, as they are very sensitive to the emotions around them. Just think: your feline friend could well be trying to tell you something.

Space clearing: putting your room through an 'energetic wash'

The more we realise how energy affects everything around us – rooms, buildings, streets, even the people who have previously occupied our bedroom – it becomes clear that 'cleansing' a space is just as important as, say, putting our clothes through the wash. Space clearing is a practice of taking care of your private space, ensuring your room, or home, is freely flowing with healthy, energetic vibes.

The space clearing steps are coming up, but first we'll take a look at why we should be applying these rituals.

What is space clearing for?

Carrying out a space clear has loads of well-being benefits when you have been feeling low or tired, or if you've just had an argument with a friend. Arguments, in particular, leave you with that horrible 'icky' feeling, so it helps to apply the space clearing rituals when you've had a negative encounter. It won't heal the argument, of course, but it will help heal the negative atmosphere around you, something that will in turn be of benefit to you.

Space clearing is also ideal if there is a particular room in the home where you feel a negative vibe, or for some reason you become sad or depressed when you go into that space. If you want to delve further, you might want to find out about the history of your home: when it was built, any notable activity, and anything about the family who lived there previously. Negative energy can linger in a building for years, as the emotional imprint is left behind when a person is unhappy, distressed or even unwell.

On a personal note, I first started to carry out these steps a few years back while at university. There was a period when I felt a strange and uncomfortable energy around me, and I knew I needed to do something about it. When you experience some-thing like this – it can be surprisingly difficult to describe – you just know through your intuition that your environment is not as it should be. I decided to look into it further and read up on the process of space clearing, which seemed the perfect remedy for my energetic woes.

You can get a professional space clearer to help sort the issue if the problem persists; however, I feel the modern goddess is more than adept at clearing away any of those negative nasties, as I like to call them. The great thing about space clearing is that it really puts a stamp on your own personal space. The person who previously lived in your home would have left their emotional mark, and so if the space isn't cleared you are being surrounded by their energetic issues.

Become the goddess of your own space by carrying out these simple steps to a healthier and happier environment:

Step 1: set your 'intention'

Decide what you wish to achieve through the space clearing. You may want to improve your mood and happiness levels, or perhaps you want an energetic fresh start after a particularly difficult few months.

You don't have to get into any kind of meditative state to set your intention, just think to yourself what it is you would like to achieve by the space clearing, and make that your goal.

Spiritual Goddess tip

The best time to carry out a space clear is when you are feeling energetic emotionally as well as physically. Save the space clearing for a day when you have nothing too pressing in your schedule. Also, wear comfortable clothing when carrying out a space clear in order that you relax and can move about the room freely. Barefoot is also best.

Step 2: grab that feather duster!

No space clear can begin without your room being in tip-top condition. When our surroundings are clean and clutter-free it helps us to feel and function that much better. A thorough top to bottom of your room will ensure the space clear gets off to a flying start.

Exercise
Clear out the clutter

1. Get rid of all those old magazines you keep under your bed but never read, clean out the dressing table of all used lipstick holders, old nail varnish bottles – you know the clutter I'm talking about. My secret, or not-so-secret, hoarding item are those free samples that come with magazines – at one point they were taking over my room!

2. It can be incredibly cathartic to throw away those items that we hoard with such fervour, and yet never actually use. By clearing the clutter you are ensuring the free flow of energy around your room.

3. Dust and clean the now clear surfaces.

For a stress-free, dust-busting clean

Turn up the volume on your favourite album – preferably one with loads of upbeat tunes to get your energy levels on a high. This exercise is all about clearing the stagnant energy, so any music that reminds you of an ex-boyfriend, for example, is an absolute no-no. The music should make you feel better, not worse.

Spiritual Goddess tip

You've just moved house … paint that space, ladies.

I understand the modern goddess rarely has a pair of overalls in her wardrobe, but if you happen to come across an old pair of leggings and a T-shirt which you would rather be seen dead in – or not as the case may be – why not start afresh in your new home by giving your room a fresh lick of paint. Now, this all depends on your situation, I realise, and the answer from the people you live with may be a resounding 'No!' The reason I suggest painting your room is not for cosmetic reasons, but a clear space is the best possible way to ensure your room is energy-happy from the get-go.

Think of your room as a blank canvas and then consider all the people who have imprinted their emotions onto your canvas: worries, stress, arguments, and so on, and you start to get a picture of how many different impressions are all over your room right now. Painting your room will ensure it has been stamped with your own signature imprint.

If painting your room is not a possibility, that is not a problem, as I have all manner of happy-inducing activities to ensure your private space is in optimum energetic condition.

Step 3: pictures/photos/posters

You want to ensure the pictures and photos that surround you reflect positivity and the great possibilities to come, which in turn can bolster your esteem.

This is also an ideal moment to put up those photos you've been meaning to sort through and frame, but have never found the time. It can enhance the environment and enjoyment of a room no end when we are surrounded by those familiar faces that always put us in a better mood.

Spiritual Goddess tip

As you start to become more spiritually aware, you will become a lot more sensitive to your surroundings, so ensure that you protect yourself regularly with your psychic bubble (page 29).

Step 4: clear the air

If you happen to have a family-free household when you carry out the space clearing, all the better; however, if your home happens to be filled with your nearest and dearest, you may want to inform them that you haven't joined a bizarre cult, but, in fact, are about to launch into Step 4 of the space clearing exercise.

Exercise
Clapping

1. Moving around your room, clapping as you go, is an effective way of releasing the stagnant, build-up of energy. The claps basically get the energy moving again. If someone was unwell in the room, or simply having a bad day, it is these imprints that leave the atmosphere around you feeling dull and heavy, so clapping is like clearing away the energetic cobwebs.

2. Always ensure the claps are strong, purposeful and with positive intent. Simply move about your room ensuring you clap around the full extent of the space. It can be quite fun to do this to music (go on, you know you want to) so if you can find a tune to complement your rhythm, by all means go for it.

If you are carrying out the space
clearing with a friend, you can task
her to help with the 'clapping' exercise.
You can also clap around electrical items such as
TVs, DVD players, and also wardrobes and the
insides of drawers. And don't forget those dusty corners where
stagnant energy builds up.

It gives a whole new meaning to the phrase 'clearing the air'.
Just think of all those large events, such as award ceremonies or
concerts where people are clapping en mass – unbeknown to
them they are taking part in a giant space-clear.

Step 5: ring that bell

The ringing of bells is the next step in the 'clear'. The most
commonly used bells for space clearing are Tibetan tingsha
bells. The bells are conveniently very small and can be obtained
from any holistic store or online; however, not to worry if you
don't happen to have those particular bells to hand (how many
of us actually do?). For this part of the exercise, you can easily
improvise with the items that can be found in the depths of your
kitchen cupboard. Although the sound won't precisely mimic
that of the bells, simply grab a metal or brass pot and a large
spoon. Now, the first time I did this I was barely able to muster
any sound louder than that of my own laughter. If anyone had
seen me walk around my bedroom clanging a spoon against a
pot, they may have come to the not so crazy conclusion that the
last marble had fallen out of the bag. I think the ultimate well-
being benefits outweigh the giggles though.

Exercise
Bell ringing

1. Ring the bells (or your improvised items) around the room.
2. Take your time with this, and ensure you have covered every inch of your room, not forgetting the space around all electrical items. In virtually no time at all, your room will be a haven of well-flowing vibes.

Step 6: aroma, aroma everywhere

Incense is perhaps the last vestige of the hippie-chic stereotype, and yet I can't enthuse enough how fabulous these little sticks are for all manner of psychic work. I did go through a phase of purchasing every type of incense I could lay my hands on and, after much experimentation, I have a few signature blends that always enhance my psychic work and meditation:

Nag champa The earthy, exotic scent of nag champa is my personal favourite, as I adore its full-bodied aroma. It is one of the most popularly used incenses in the world, and an excellent accompaniment to meditation and connecting with your angelic/spirit guides. It is the 'little black dress' of the incense world: a must-have for any incense wardrobe.

Sandalwood The woody aroma of sandalwood is ideal for space clearing purposes as it is used for its purifying and cleansing benefits. It has a lovely calming effect also, so if you feel you need to clear your room of any negative build up, such as a recent argument that occurred in the space, sandalwood can help restore the balance and calm the atmosphere around you.

Frankincense This is the one I personally use for space clearing purposes, and it also doubles up as the perfect aroma for stress relief too. I like to have frankincense in the background while I carry out a space clear, as I know it is working towards helping me achieve the end 'cleansed' result. This one is also ideal to use while meditating, as it has a very soothing quality.

Jasmine The 'sensual' aroma of jasmine is the ideal incense to burn when setting the scene for that special, romantic visit. My tip is to burn for 10–15 minutes before your intended arrives so that there is a subtle sexy aroma flowing through your room. A perfect incense choice for a loved-up evening with the boyfriend.

Experiment with the different types of incense until you find the blend that best suits your personal requirements.

If you find several blends that you like, you can even match up the different scents for specific psychic activities. For instance, you may have a blend that you burn only when manifesting or space clearing, and another when speaking with your angels. This is a very good practice as you start to create a ritual for your angelic communication, particularly when linking with your Guardian Angel.

One word of caution: be careful to extinguish the stick after using, and always place the incense holder on a secure ledge. You don't want to ignite any twin flames of the wrong sort.

Step 7: to the kitchen cupboard!

The condiments upon your kitchen unit may not initially strike you as items used in a space clearing, and yet one of the more popular methods of clearing includes salt, which is an important component of the overall energy cleanse. From your kitchen shopping list you will need sea salt and four bowls.

Exercise
Cleansing with salt

1. Pour a generous amount of salt into each bowl, and place in the corners of the room. Stale energy has a sneaky habit of gathering in those poky corners, so it is the ideal location for the bowls.
2. The salt will soak up the negative energy, so it is advisable to keep the bowls there all day. Just remember not to reuse the salt, and throw away once finished.

Step 8: let there be light

To bring the space clear to an end, you can take a moment to surround your home with the protective bubble of light.

Exercise
Ending the space clear with light

1. All you need to do is close your eyes and picture your home in your mind's eye, and now see it being bathed in a beautiful protective white light, and see that light form a bubble around your home, which will keep it safe and protected.
2. For an added boost, you can assign an angel or archangel to oversee the protection of your home.

Spirituallly Cleanse Your Home   153

An additional space clearing tip

Fresh flowers or plants look lovely in the bedroom and enhance the space clearing process. The problem with hand-picked flowers is that they can be a lot of bother and wilt rather quickly, so you may want to invest in a small house plant that requires minimum time and effort. If you do happen to be a fresh-flower girl, make sure you remove them from your bedroom as soon as they have passed their best.

Exercise
The speedy space clear

If you happen to be pushed for time, why not try the fast-track to energetic harmony with this speedy space clear:

1. Clap your hands around the room, especially in those corners.
2. Open all the windows in your room.
3. Play some uplifting music that helps to put you in a better frame of mind.
4. Incense: you only need to burn for 5 minutes and then extinguish the stick.
5. Surround yourself and your room with your protective psychic bubble.

This will take only 5–10 minutes max, and is ideal for the busy goddess who has a million and one things to do, and only 5 minutes to spare.

Space clearing

The process of cleansing a room or house in order to establish a free-flow of clean, happy energy.

Be your own interior designer

Look around your bedroom and think about what you want your space to reflect. We all have a natural tendency to fill our room with whatever items we happen to have or are given along the way. It inevitably starts to pile up – never a good look for creating a harmonious sanctuary. Start to think of your room as a reflection of who you are and not merely a dumping ground for your 'stuff'. Think about what makes you happy and what you would like to be surrounded by. It can be useful to make a list of the things in life that inspire and make you feel good. Think about colours, textures and scents. Just a few simple changes can totally transform a space.

Ideas for a perfect room

- ◆ Fabulous scented candles
- ◆ Pictures from past holidays
- ◆ Favourite books by the bedside
- ◆ Inspiring quotes that uplift and inspire

Your bedroom should be a sanctuary of peace and tranquillity where you can just 'be'. Altering your current space need not be a costly experiment either; in fact, you probably have many of the items already but just haven't found the time to organise them. And you can always pick up items along the way. Why not create a wish list of all those items you have spotted – that gorgeous throw, for example, which you think would look stunning over your bedspread? Over time, you will start to create the ultimate goddess retreat.

That extra-special space

Create that special place in your home, or 'sacred space', as it is often called: your own private corner assigned for meditation purposes, manifesting, or simply chilling with your angelic guides.

If you have a space in your room which up until now has been used as storage space for boxes, this may be a good time to reassign them a home, and start creating a space specifically for your psychic work. The sacred space doesn't have to be a large area, just as long as you can sit or lie comfortably. You can create a cosy atmosphere with throws, blankets and cushions – comfort is the priority in this space. Surround yourself with photographs of your loved ones, pictures that inspire you, and beautiful candles. It should be an indulgence of the senses of all the things you cherish and adore. Crystals are also another wonderful way of charging the space with their powerful and energetic vibes (more on crystal matters in the next chapter).

As this special place is designed for you and all your goddess-inspired work, make sure you keep it protected with your trusty bubble. The psychic bubble is not just for your personal protection but can also be used to protect your home, even your most treasured possessions. Why not protect this most sacred of spaces to ensure it remains the truly inspired part of your home?

Spiritual Goddess tip

If you've just had an argument with a friend or boyfriend, make sure that you conduct a mini space clear after they have left. Arguments not only affect us on an emotional level but on an energetic level too, so remember to cleanse the space.

Your work is done

All things that go bump in the night are rarely as they seem. Something that first appears as a spooky happening can ultimately be cast in a far more forgiving light once we become energetically savvy about our surroundings.

If the modern goddess can continually spread her light, understanding, and perfectly shiny energetic vibes, it can lead the way for others who are still hiding beneath the covers.

The Goddess Hour

*Y*ou've just prepared yourself for a night out with the girls: lipstick applied, hair styled, outfit chosen. You should be feeling your very best, and yet, despite all your sartorial efforts, you just don't feel like your usual self.

Anxiety, stress and all manner of nerve-jangling situations can cause havoc in our emotional life, and make even the most fun night out with friends seem more like an evening chore. The most glammed-up exterior, after all, can't hide how we truly feel on the inside.

If you start to sense you're fast approaching stress overload, it is important to address these imbalances right away and factor in some time for 'self' healing. This is the moment to indulge in all those activities that help bring you back to full restorative glory.

The ongoing to-do list of life, after all, never ends, and your personal time is of equal importance to your work and indeed your social life. Having a moment to just 'be' is where your spiritual self really starts to kick in.

This chapter will look into all manner of stress-relieving practices and demonstrates how even the most frazzled of goddesses can become a picture of Zen-like tranquillity.

Meditation (time to exhale)

Just hearing the word 'meditation' has the kind of soothing resonance which will come as sweet relief for today's non-stop goddess. The ancient technique of meditation is as relevant now as it has ever been and, with regular practice, it will take you off to a place of centred serenity – or at least as serene as your daily schedule permits.

I came upon meditation many years ago during something of a stressed period of my life. Friends and family were quick to inject their advice, and were more than forthcoming with their thoughts on the matter. I started to detect, however, a pattern in their little 'pep talks' and noticed how the word 'meditation' was being used with alarming regularity. It appeared to me that meditation had become the new byword for chill out/take time for yourself/just relax and so on. And so I took it as a universal sign to find out if this 'meditation' was indeed the answer to my stressing situation.

The first time I attended a meditation group I actually fell asleep – too many comfy cushions, it was bound to happen. It had me thinking whether meditation was, in fact, just one lovely long excuse to catch up on some much-needed shut-eye, but after managing to stay awake for the following class, I realised it had a lot more to offer when you manage to remain 'in the moment'.

What is meditation?

Meditation is like taking a mini holiday from your hectic life, and although you don't physically travel to some exotic location, your mind is otherwise engaged in a blissful sojourn of rest and relaxation. Meditation, to that effect, is used for all manner of stress-related issues:

◆ Problems with concentration
◆ Stress in home/work life
◆ Feeling tearful and anxious
◆ Being unable to sleep

What happens when we meditate?

Here's the 'technical' bit! When we meditate, we switch off from our busy, 'I've got so much to do' way of thinking, otherwise known as the beta wavelength, and switch to the ever so relaxed alpha.

Beta This highly functional state of being usually begins when we leave the home in the morning, and finishes when our sleepy head hits the pillow at night. This is our 'survival mode', as we endeavour to deal with all manner of situations the day brings: family issues, work stress, trying to organise that girlie holiday – all these activities have us programmed to our highly functional beta wavelength.

The beta wavelength is finally silenced when we achieve:

Alpha, aka the ahhh moment! This blissful state of being occurs when we are at our most relaxed and creative. It is a pleasurable state to be in and comes about during meditation or when we are doing something we really enjoy. With regular meditation, you will have the alpha programmed into your mental speed dial.

When you meditate, you link with your Higher Self, otherwise known as your spiritual self, as discussed earlier in the book. If you meditate on a regular basis you will be able to let go more easily of any worries and issues, and will notice how positive thought will become a bigger part of your everyday thinking.

Lotus position optional (bendy legs required!)

I once tried to get into the infamous lotus position to meditate – big mistake. Not only did my legs cramp up in ways I never thought possible but it also left me in the most unrelaxed, unmeditative state I could imagine. For those goddesses who will only endure pain in their legs for those beloved strappy heels (like me), here are a few positions that are more conducive to instant relaxation:

- ◆ Sitting cross-legged on the floor, propped up by lovely soft cushions.
- ◆ Lying down with your arms either side.
- ◆ Sitting upright, hands rested on your lap and feet firmly on the ground.
- ◆ You can even meditate as you are now. Just remember: comfort is meditation's best friend.

Spiritual Goddess tip

If any part of your body feels uncomfortable while meditating, always change your position. You don't want to spend the entire session aware of your discomfort.

Get started with the listening meditation

Let's have a go at meditating, with one of my personal favourites. This meditation is ideal if you are just starting out and want to try a technique that is fuss-free and really effective.

The listening meditation is designed to help us switch off from our non-stop internal chatter – our 'inner dialogue'. At this very moment, we are all narrating our past, present and even future experiences. This chatter, for the most part, helps us to sort through our thoughts and decisions. On the flip side, it can also have a detrimental effect on our self-esteem. How many of us have decided not to wear our favourite outfit because we felt self-conscious about it? The likelihood is that our internal chatter talked us out of it. This is where a listening meditation comes in and is the perfect antidote when we need to quiet our minds and keep focused on simply 'being in the moment'.

Most meditations are designed to shut off from the external world, and yet our internal world can be just as loud. If your personal narrator is starting to wear you out, this is the perfect meditation for you.

Exercise
Listening meditation

1. Sit or lie down in a secluded location where you have time to observe your surroundings without being disturbed. I prefer to keep my eyes open while going through this meditation, but closed is fine if you prefer.

2. Take a moment to ground yourself (page 28), as it's good practice to include this in all meditative exercises. Also, do make sure that you are in a comfortable position, and that you're warm enough.

I can't tell you how many times I have had to break in the middle of a meditation because I suddenly realised the room was freezing, so always keep a blanket close by.

3. Once you have settled and feel comfortable, start to focus your attention on simply 'listening' to your environment. It may be the hum of the television downstairs, the sounds of the home, or simply the rhythm of your own breathing. By 'tuning in' to what you can hear in your external environment, you are effectively 'tuning out' of your internal dialogue.

4. Don't worry if any thoughts suddenly pop into your mind, it's bound to happen. The best thing to do is acknowledge the thought, and then simply let it drift away.

5. It can be incredibly calming to just observe your surroundings, knowing that that is your only task during the meditation. Stay concentrated on listening and it's surprising how quickly you stop hearing your own thoughts.

6. You can carry out this meditation for 5 minutes, or longer if you are enjoying the experience. It's the quality of the time that's important, not just the quantity. If you feel after several minutes you have really benefited from the 'moment', it has been a meditation well spent.

7. When you have come to the end of the meditation, remember to 'ground' yourself.

Further meditations are coming up later in the chapter.

When do I meditate?

Many people ask how long and how often you should meditate. It really all depends on you. If you find that meditation is your 'thing', practise every day if you can find the time. Before you head out in the morning, why not factor in a quick 5–10 minutes and make it part of your daily routine? For others, it may be once a week, whereas some people may choose to meditate when they are going through periods of stress and need to try many different activities to bring about a state of calm.

As you practise meditating, vary it to your personal requirements. There is no hard-and-fast rule that meditation has to adhere to any specific guidelines. You can mix it up by having some music in the background, or try meditating with a specific blend of incense if that helps you get out of your everyday state and into blissful relaxation.

Meditation

Taking time to switch off from the world around to concentrate on 'you'. It has plenty of well-being benefits, as it helps you to de-stress and get back to a more harmonious state of being.

Crystals

The modern girl is usually equipped with the following: lipstick (of course), mobile, keys, card, mints – any of these sound familiar? You may want to consider another potential contender for the inner depths of your favourite handbag: the shiny, sparkling and gorgeous crystal is the modern goddess's secret weapon for 21st-century living.

Crystals have been used for literally thousands of years for their full-to-the-brim healing properties. These little gems can help heal our aura, balance our chakras and even provide a little boost in the love department. It will please you to know that even the most stressing of issues can be helped with the aid of crystals.

How do crystals work?

Our energetic self is picking up and responding to energy all the time – crystals too have an energetic vibration to them, which is why they have such a beneficial effect on our aura. Crystals transmit their healing vibes, which help us on an emotional, physical and spiritual level. They have hundreds of uses for our modern-day issues: you may be feeling stressed, anxious, or even lovesick – crystal to the rescue, I say. All crystals, no matter how big or small, have powerful energetic properties, and help us at a subconscious level, so all that healing goodness is taking effect even if we may not be able to sense it straight away.

What are crystals used for?

Crystals are used for all manner of purposes, including: healing, meditation, stress relief – and even as gorgeous accessories. These multi-faceted sparklers can do no wrong, and can help in all kinds of life situations:

- ◆ Enhance the love life – try rose quartz
- ◆ Lacking in creativity – try orange carnelian
- ◆ Learning to forgive – try lapis lazuli
- ◆ Meditation – try smoky quartz
- ◆ Stamina and endurance – try orange calcite
- ◆ Feeling sad or uninspired – try blue lace agate
- ◆ Unwell and in need of an immune boost – try red jasper
- ◆ Fear of flying – try smoky quartz
- ◆ Determination to achieve your ambitions – try tiger's eye
- ◆ Important exams coming up – try citrine
- ◆ Enhance your psychic skills – try amethyst

Choosing the crystal which is right for you

All crystals are fabulous, but I tend to think the crystal chooses the person it is meant to help, and so choosing a crystal should be a very organic process. You can of course buy crystals online if you are after something specific, but I think there is nothing better than going into a holistic shop and spending some time looking at the crystals, then getting a tangible sense of what you like and what you feel drawn to. In shops where crystals are sold, they are generally laid out on a table where you can easily handle them in order to find the stone that is the right shape and size for you.

I suggest placing your hand just above the crystals, and then gently scanning along and feeling the vibrations you pick up. You may sense a tingly sensation in your palm or over the tips of your fingers, perhaps hot or cold spots. We all pick up on energy differently, so learn to trust what you feel. If you sense you want your hand to stop or you feel there is a specific crystal that is 'calling out to you', go with that instinct; the crystal you come upon may be the crystal you need at that moment in your life. I have included an in-depth guide on page 167 of some of the more popular crystals to help you get started. Happy crystal shopping!

How do I get the most out my crystals?

The most convenient way of getting the most out of your crystal is by wearing it as jewellery. There are all manner of beautiful necklaces, bracelets and rings that contain crystal. You may have seen people wear those huge pieces of crystal either on a necklace or a ring, but I can assure you that size really doesn't matter when it comes to crystals – even the smaller ones have very powerful healing properties.

Of course, you may not want to wear crystal jewellery all the time, so simply carry a small piece of crystal in a pouch and keep it with you as you go about your day.

Or, if you have time, you can try a more intensive crystal meditation. For the meditation, you can use any crystal you wish (please see the Crystal Guide on the next page for an in-depth guide to their properties) depending on what you are hoping to achieve.

Exercise
Crystal meditation

1. Find a quiet spot in your room to carry out the meditation, such as your sacred space. You can sit up or lie down for this exercise, just as long as you can see your crystal clearly. Once you have found a comfortable position, ground (page 28) and apply your psychic protection (page 29).

2. Place your crystal in the palm of your hand and spend a few moments becoming familiar with it. Look at its shape, colour and texture. Take in every detail so that you can picture it clearly in your mind.

3. Close your eyes and clasp your fingers around the crystal so that it is nestled snugly in the palm of your hand.

4. Start to visualise the crystal in your mind, and allow it to become the central focus of the meditation.

5. Spend a few moments thinking about its texture, unique individual shape and the depth of its colour. Enjoy recreating the image of your crystal in your mind.

6. If any stray thoughts enter into your mind, acknowledge them briefly and then send them on their way. Keep your focus on the crystal and, as you do, you may start to receive further images coming into focus.

7. Are you seeing more vibrant colours or different images of the crystal? Allow yourself to go with the visual you are receiving and enjoy the sensation however subtle it may be to begin with. The more you practise, the stronger the visual will become.
8. Spend 5 minutes or longer enjoying the crystal meditation.
9. When you feel you have come to the end of the meditation, open your eyes and gently come to by grounding.

Crystal guide

All crystals have multi-healing benefits, and I've highlighted some of their more popular uses:

Amethyst (purple) The multi-tasker of the crystal world, amethyst is particularly beneficial in times of emotional stress. It can help aid a good night's rest, and is perfect for developing psychic awareness. Amethyst is good to have around when you are carrying out a space-clearing exercise, particularly when placed around electrical items such as TVs and computers.

Azurite (blue) The stone of 'awareness', azurite is one which is often used to help open the third eye chakra, aka your psychic ability. This beautiful stone assists with greater clarity and focus, and its soothing presence makes it a lovely crystal to work with, particularly at the beginning of your psychic development.

Orange Calcite I am sure we would all be in some kind of psychic agreement when I say that shopping, of any kind, is exhausting work. Exhaustion and tiredness are things we can all relate to, and if you're suffering from shopping or any other related fatigue, orange calcite will help you call upon those extra energy reserves.

Clear Quartz (transparent) This ultimate healing crystal can instantly empower and enhance any psychic work, as well as helping you work on any emotional issues you may be experiencing. This crystal is particularly handy to have around if you have been feeling unwell, and it will give an extra boost to the healing process.

Lapis Lazuli (blue with gold flecks) Of all the crystals, lapis is the one I tend to think has something of the wow factor about it. The vibrant blue, speckled with gold, is so stunning it has you in its power from the moment you see it. Thankfully, lapis is as good on the inside as it is on the outside. Above all, it is known as the 'friendship' crystal, as it helps to break down barriers in order that you can create deeper and more meaningful relationships.

Blue Lace Agate This beautiful, pale blue stone has an air of tranquillity from the moment you place it in the palm of your hand. This stone has a protective, nurturing quality, which is beneficial if you feel stressed or vulnerable in any way. It is like that fabulous friend who brings around their love and understanding (and a girlie flick) when you are feeling low. It is a lovely, comforting crystal to have around at any time.

Citrine (yellow) The cheery, sunny disposition of citrine represents all-round happiness and good vibes. To keep your mood levels up, citrine will happily sit in your pocket emanating those sun-filled vibes they are most famous for. Citrine is also fabulous to have around if you need to keep your focus and concentration levels up – perfect if you have upcoming exams or are embarking on an extensive work project.

Tiger's Eye (shimmering brown/gold) Along with the amethyst, the tiger's eye is another one of my personal favourite crystals. The colour has a tiger-like quality with its deep shimmering brown and gold. Keep the tiger's eye close if you are embarking on a new phase in your life, in which you need to find strength and courage. The energy from this stone will help you to keep your focus and, most importantly, will keep your confidence sky high.

Red Jasper The psychic bubble you surround yourself with can be given extra support with the help of red jasper. This remarkable crystal can ward off the negative energy that surrounds us daily, particularly if you regularly travel on public transport. The crystal also has a healing effect on the aura, so it is perfect to keep around during any aura maintenance.

Bloodstone (dark green with red flecks) At the start of any kind of psychic work there is a preliminary grounding (page 28) and psychic protection (page 29) exercise. Bloodstone is ideal for this kind of work, so keep it by your side or in the palm of your hand as you start to ground yourself. Bloodstone is also perfect for meditative work, so you can place it on a ledge nearby or hold it if you prefer.

Jade If you feel you are on the fast track to worry overload, and your emotional self is teetering on the brink, the crystal you might like to try is jade. This pale green crystal helps you to find more balance, and a greater sense of peace within yourself. As the name also suggests, the soothing green is very calming to observe, and incredibly pretty too.

Malachite (dark green) The powerful malachite is a true 'cleansing' stone, and can help us deal with those negative emotions that may have been festering away for some time. Not all emotional baggage is so easy to deal with, and some of our issues take a little extra time to sort through. Malachite can help you to address and then release those issues.

Orange Carnelian The career-minded goddess would do well to keep a piece of orange carnelian for those periods of increased work-driven focus. It is the perfect crystal for helping you to realise your ambitions. Also, if you are starting to actively manifest, orange carnelian can help you visualise, and should be kept close to your ultimate wish list.

Angelite (pale blue/white) If connecting with the angelic realm is something you are starting to work towards, the process can be enhanced even further with angelite. This crystal is used extensively to help strengthen the connection with the angels. It is a stone that is powerful, yet has an aura of such grace and gentleness it is like being held in the safest place imaginable. It's a truly beautiful crystal.

Rose Quartz (pale pink) The ultimate in all things 'love' related, whether it be the love between family and friends or the one that makes you swoon, rose quartz can help deepen these connections even further. This stone is also one of compassion, not only for those closest but also to the world around us. It is also the sweetest pink hue you'll ever see.

Smoky Quartz (clear/pale grey) If you have been holding on to a fear or concern for a while, and your thoughts have been distracted and clouded with worry, the smoky quartz crystal will help you break free of these fears. We're human, and we all worry, so keeping this ultra-healing crystal close by will help to clear away concerns and doubt.

Yellow Jasper Our imagination and ideas can get a little extra creative inspiration with the help of yellow jasper. A new venture or idea can often be tricky to realise, so keep a piece of this lovely yellow crystal to inspire you further, and ignite your creativity. This crystal also helps dispel any negative energy, and will keep you protected as you pursue your dreams.

As you may have guessed, I'm pretty much infatuated with them all. If you told me to choose (do I really have to?) I would probably favour the amethyst and tiger's eye. Once you get acquainted with the crystals, however, I have a sneaking suspicion you may find yourself in the same dilemma – it's impossible to have just one favourite.

Chakras and their corresponding crystals

- ◆ Crown (purple/white) – amethyst or clear quartz
- ◆ Third eye (indigo) – lapis lazuli or azurite
- ◆ Throat (blue) – blue lace agate or angelite
- ◆ Heart (pink/green) – rose quartz or jade
- ◆ Solar plexus (yellow) – citrine or yellow jasper
- ◆ Sacral (orange) – orange carnelian or orange calcite
- ◆ Root (red) – red jasper or tiger's eye (tiger's eye is not specifically of the corresponding colour, but a fabulous crystal nonetheless to help balance your root chakra)

Crystals to heal your chakras

Crystals can be used to heal the chakras, and are even more effective when they are of the corresponding colour; for example, if you feel that your heart chakra requires a little extra attention you can try wearing rose quartz on a necklace so the crystal is hanging close to the heart centre. As this chakra also has the colour green, you could also try jade.

You can also meditate while holding the crystal of your choice, and visualise your chakras being healed (a chakra meditation is on the way).

The one, the only, 'I'm practically perfect': amethyst

If you are looking for that elusive multi-tasker, the ultimate crystal that can tackle all manner of emotional hotspots, and still look gorgeous on your bedside table, you need look no further than the amethyst.

The amethyst is something of a shining superstar of the crystal world. It can help you open up your crown chakra and access all that spiritual knowledge just waiting to flood in. The amethyst also assists with any kind of emotional issue, and helps even out our moods. And for those goddesses who are a magnet for other people's emotional problems, it will help keep you safe and protected.

I actually have a lovely little piece of amethyst sitting next to me as I type, as it's one of my personal favourites. Just looking at its deep purple hue sends me to a place of spiritual tranquillity. Gotta love the amethyst!

Spiritual Goddess tip

For the ultimate bath treat, put some of your favourite crystals in a bowl and place them around the room – bath time has never been this good.

How to clean your crystal

Crystals, like people, take on the negative energy of others and can get frazzled and run down quite easily. If you have just purchased a crystal, it is advisable to cleanse it before use, as the crystal would have been handled by many people in the shop, so you want to ensure your crystal is in optimum condition before its first use.

There are many ways in which to care for your crystal:

Sunlight Your crystal is put on 'energetic charge' when left out in the natural light. If you have a garden, find a location where you can carefully place the crystal, without the cat deciding it's found a new toy, that is. Or, if you have a small balcony or ledge where you can safely place the crystal, that is fine too. You can leave the crystal out for as long as you like – ideally, for at least a day.

Water seems the most natural way of cleansing a crystal, and it is certainly one of the most effective. Simply hold the crystal in the palm of your hand and put it under running water. Before you do this, make sure that your crystal is suitable to immerse in water. Certain crystals don't take well to water, such as azurite, lapis lazuli, malachite, angelite and orange calcite, so double-check before you wash them. Alternatively, you can simply apply your 'intention' as outlined below.

Intention If you don't have time to give your crystals their own personal shower, you can always apply the simplest ritual of all for cleansing these little beauties. Place your crystal(s) in the palm of your hand and apply your 'intention' by visualising them cleansed of all negative energy. Surround your crystals with white light, and visualise them immersed in your ever faithful, psychic bubble. And *voilà*! Your instant route to the cleanest crystals around.

How to look after your crystal when out and about

Ideally, you should keep your crystal in a small pouch, so as not to damage it in any way. Also, be careful of how you handle your crystal. It's lovely to share crystals with friends, of course; however, if too many people start handling your crystal it will be picking up on their energies. So if you've had something of a crystal 'show and tell' with your friends, make sure you apply the cleansing rituals before using again, and place it back in its safe little pouch.

You and 'your' crystal

Choosing a crystal should be an intuitive decision, and one that should be a natural fit between the two of you. You may go through a phase of trying to decide which crystal is right for you, and this is a valuable practice, as you can work out which crystal energy is ideal for your specific needs.

Once you have chosen your crystal, and started working with it through meditation, you will quickly attune to its energy and a special synergy will form between the two of you – a bit like a friend really. If you treat your shining little gem (and friend) with respect and care, you will receive that same vibrant energy back.

Bag that crystal

If you can't find the time to squeeze in a crystal meditation, always know that you can get the wonderful healing vibes of your crystal, courtesy of your favourite handbag. Before you head out in the morning, place a piece of your favourite crystal in a safe compartment, and those healing energies will be with you all day.

Also, if you are heading home for a quick change before a night out with friends or a hot date, you may want to swap the crystal, depending on your mood. In no time at all, you will be working those positive vibes into your social and crystal life.

Colour

The different qualities that crystals possess are also connected to the colours we discussed in the aura and chakra colour guides. Without a doubt, colour has an important role to play in our day-to-day lives – it has the power to uplift, inspire, excite and even tantalise. It can also leave us feeling rather 'blue', particularly on those grey days when we don't even want to open the curtains.

Colour can make us feel so many different emotions as, like everything else, it has a vibration. Wearing the colour red, for example, will have you feeling totally different from, say, the colour yellow. Red is the ultimate in sassy and confident dressing; equally, the colour yellow is known for being cheery, optimistic and full of those sunny, laid-back vibes that everyone seems to gravitate to.

The shades and hues in which we choose to colour our life say much about the kind of person we are, and what we want to project to the world.

If you are currently experiencing something of a colour déjà vu, and the same serial offenders keep showing up in your wardrobe, it may be time for a colour make-over.

I hope the following may galvanise your ideas on colour. For a further in-depth colour analysis, see the Colour Guide in Chapter 3.

Your colour life

I want to:

... feel re-energised and back to my usual fabulous self.

Red is the colour of passion, power, sexiness and vibrancy. You don't have to swamp your wardrobe with red; simply choose statement pieces such as a hat or belt that you can mix and match with most of your outfits. I'm sure I've mentioned this earlier, but don't forget that slick of red lipstick – it works wonders, ladies.

... access my ultimate spiritual goddess.

Purple is *the* spiritual colour, hands down. Have you ever noticed in holistic stores how purple is usually the dominant colour? This isn't by accident. All the hues of the purple spectrum open up the spiritual, intuitive goddess within. If purple is not your colour of choice, an amethyst crystal is a perfect accessory, and gives you all the purple vibes you need.

... feel connected to my mysterious, sexy side.

Black denotes the ultimate in power dressing, and looks exquisite on any goddess. This colour is also one of mystery and sophistication – what guy could possibly resist! The LBD (little black dress), after all, is a perennial staple of any wardrobe and never goes out of style.

... invigorate my life without the need for caffeine.

Try incorporating the citrusy yellow. Yellow is a cheerful colour and one that signifies optimism and enthusiasm. Yellow also helps you to see things more clearly, so if you have been wearing colours that have you yawning and reaching for your pillow, yellow should start to liven things up a bit!

... feel more calm and serene (less panicky).

A simple white shirt/top, teamed with a piece of blue lace agate on a silver chain, will have you as close to serene as the modern goddess can get. White is a spiritual colour, and blue exudes calm, so the two combined is a dream combination. If you feel that your panicky nature needs an extra shot of serenity, try including more regular 'space clearing' into your schedule.

... become more inspired by life and have the drive to pursue what I want to do.

Orange is known for its energising qualities, and a colour that can invigorate even the most tired and jaded of wardrobes. Orange is also associated with drive and determination, and can help ignite the wherewithal to help you stay motivated as you work towards achieving your goals.

... feel a greater sense of balance, and not go from one extreme to the other (a need for 'inner' calm).

Green is *the* colour for 'balance' and keeping a clear-headed perspective on matters. It is probably no surprise that green is the 'nature' colour, which in itself has all the restorative vibes of a reviving walk in a park. Keep your calm with any shade of green, and try a piece of jade crystal for an extra healing boost.

... impress on a first date and achieve that perfect mix of gorgeous, sexy and sophisticated.

Try mixing your colours with a soft feminine pink, which is the colour of love and compassion. Black, as you know, brings out your sexy side, and looks oh so sophisticated.
Again, it doesn't have to be in giant blocks of colour – try a simple black top with a rose quartz necklace, and see if that works for you.

Colour should always be an expression of 'you', and an intuitive decision on your behalf. If you feel a certain colour isn't working, always trust your inner voice, and be guided by what you think and not the current fashion trends. All colours can be integrated into your own personal style. Colour, after all, never goes out of fashion.

Spiritual Goddess tip

If you are feeling low on energy, change the colour of your current outfit to that which you wish your 'inner' self to reflect. You may want to feel calmer and so switch to light blue – watch how your mood changes.

Colour and your surroundings

Colour doesn't just apply to our clothing or accessories, it's also important to think of colour in every aspect of life, particularly our work spaces where we spend much of our time. A work space where you have your laptop and phone, for example, may be an area where you need to feel particularly energised. Think about the items where colour can be included:

Laptop Ensure your screensaver invigorates you from the moment you switch it on in the morning. Choose bright, zesty colours such as orange and yellow.

Crystals are great around the work space and can be placed close to electrical items such as laptops. Amethyst and clear quartz are perfect for this. Also, smoky quartz is ideal for better communication, so keep a piece near your computer and phone to help keep the flow.

Plants are brilliant around the work space, and you can even put a crystal inside the pot to help energise them. The green of the plant is balancing and brings a bit of nature to your desk.

Look in front of you What do you see when you remove your gaze from the screen of your computer? If you don't happen to have the most inspiring vista, think about how you can enhance your environment with colour. Pictures, photos, posters can all be used to enhance your space and keep your energy levels up. Think about the colours that will be most conducive to a more happy and positive you.

The zesty colours naturally keep us energised; however, if you decide the feeling you want to create is to be more serene, think about using pale blues and pinks. Slight adjustments to your environment need not cost the earth, but they go a long way towards helping keep your work space colour-happy.

Exercise
A colourful meditation

For an extra colour boost, you can work on a chakra meditation to spice things up in your colour life. If you want to work on a specific chakra, don't forget your crystal.

If you have created a sacred space (see Chapter 7) this would be the perfect location to carry out the meditation. If not, find a quiet place where you won't be disturbed and begin by grounding (page 28) and then apply the psychic protection (page 29).

1. **Root** Close your eyes and visualise the root chakra (base of spine). Visualise the chakra exactly how it comes to you, whether it be the shape of a wheel or a ball of colour; I actually see the chakra

as a sphere shape, but allow the visual to come in the way that feels right to you. Take as much time as you need until you feel you have the visual clearly in your mind.

Imagine the chakra glowing a vibrant red and then allow the colour to fill your entire body, focusing particularly around the root and right down through your legs to the tips of your toes.

2. **Sacral** From the root we move up the chakras to the sacral (just below your navel), and start to visualise the glowing, vibrant orange of the sacral filling your entire being with colour. Keep your main focus around your navel area to allow the healing colour to work its magic.

3. **Solar Plexus** Carry on up the chakras to the solar plexus (stomach area), which when healthy will be a golden yellow colour. I also want to point out that if you feel particularly drawn to a chakra, stay with the visual longer, as it may be that the chakra needs a little extra TLC. Allow the healing colour to circulate around your stomach area with a warm golden glow.

4. **Heart** Travelling up from the solar plexus you will come to the pink/green hue of the heart chakra (chest). If you find it difficult to envisage both colours at the same time, stick with the colour that comes to you more easily, in order that you can create the most vibrant visual possible. Allow the healing colours to have your heart chakra glowing with healthy, loving vibes.

5. **Throat** Moving up, you'll come to the sky blue of the throat chakra (neck). The blue should expand far beyond the neck area, in order that the clear blue is working on your 'communicative' chakra.

6. **Third eye** You're almost at the top now (it will be worth it) and you'll arrive at your psychic portal, aka your third eye chakra. Visualise the deep indigo colour, and allow this colour to expand. See the colour in the space between your eyes, which is where your third eye chakra is located. Time spent nurturing and developing this chakra will continually progress your psychic development.

7. **Crown** Right at the top you will reach your crown chakra (top of the head). The pure white light should flood through your crown, right through to the base of your feet, filling your whole body,

expanding as far as you can imagine. The colour purple is also associated with the crown so, if you can, visualise the two colours joining together – a very potent spiritual mix. Allow the colours to wash through your entire body, and keep with this healing colour for as long as you can.

Once you feel your visual has come to an end, slowly bring yourself back into the room, open your eyes, rub your hands together, and take a sip of water to help you ground.

Chakra, colour, clothing ...

Colour can be strategically placed to enhance and aid healthy, happy chakras. Simply use the colour that corresponds with the particular chakra, and refer to the Chakra Guide (Chapter 3) to refresh your memory. To give you a quick idea of how you can mix and match, see my clothing chakra/colour rundown with a few ideas you might like to try:

Head Accessorise with a purple/white hat or headband. You can even use purple/white hair clips (suitable for goddesses of any age).

Neck Try a sky-blue necklace such as blue lace agate or lapis lazuli to help with better communication. Looking after this chakra will also help you to express your ideas and dreams more clearly, which is important when manifesting.

Torso A green/pink top helps to keep a healthy heart chakra. You can incorporate these colours particularly in times of stress, or when you're head over heels in love.

Waist Choose a belt with a splash of yellow to keep your solar plexus on an even keel. If bright yellow doesn't quite make you jump for joy, find a belt which subtly integrates the colour without being too bold.

Legs Your sacral and root chakras can be enhanced further with a dash of orange/red. Perhaps you have a great red skirt or a pair of tights you've been meaning to wear – this would be the perfect opportunity to try something new, and it helps your well-being too.

We are surrounded by colour at every moment, and yet it's rarely something we give much 'spiritual' thought to. We see a dress in a shop and we instantly feel compelled to have it – is it the cut, the sexy neckline, or could it be that we are unconsciously drawn to the colour because a specific chakra is in need of a little colour TLC? Next time you're out and about, think about your current emotional life and consider which colours can help you to feel that much better. It may be that the outfit you choose could be giving you not only an aesthetic boost but also more well-being benefits than meet the eye. I guarantee you'll be the most colour-savvy goddess in the store.

Spiritual Goddess tip

If you are unsure about wearing a certain colour, gradually start to introduce it into your wardrobe via jewellery, shoes or even a handbag. As you get more confident with the colour, you can start to make it a more regular feature of your wardrobe.

Goddess is good to go

The feeling of being connected to your 'self' is perhaps the most relevant lesson for the modern goddess today. After all, what could be more empowering than taking control of your own spiritual well-being?

Whatever it is that helps you feel like 'you' is the kind of spiritual medicine we should all be taking at least once a day. It may involve meditation, crystals, invigorating the colour of your wardrobe or even chatting to a close girlfriend.

That perfect spiritual–material balance is there for the taking and is one that, in time, will set you apart as the 'ultimate' spiritual goddess.

One Last Thing. . .

I remember when I first opened up about my interest in the mystical and spiritual aspect of life. I knew it was always going to divide opinion and certainly ignite some sparky conversation, but on the whole, people were wonderfully open-minded and happy to share their experiences and thoughts on the matter. I also became accustomed to the 'other' kind of response, which usually involved the terrified expression of someone who thought I was about to whip out my crystal ball and so predict the next 20 years of their life. It makes me laugh now, as we have become so much more savvy than that, and thank goodness.

As the sisterhood of a new spiritual generation, we are aware of the spiritual 'self' and yet don't neglect our material life. Spirituality, after all, is just one aspect of the greater mix of everything life has to offer – why can't we enjoy going out with friends, fall madly in love, argue, cry, laugh, make a huge mistake, be boring, be happy, have a great day, have a bad day – and still be spiritual?

In reading this book, I hope it has set you on your path to discovering your own inner goddess.

Stephanie x

Acknowledgements

Many people have helped bring this book together and I would like to thank them all. First of all, I would like to say a big thank you to Piatkus for all their fabulous work. I would like to pay very special thanks to my editor, Rebecca Woods, who has been nothing short of my publishing guardian angel, making it the most wonderful experience any author could wish for. Zoe Goodkin and Claudia Dyer for guiding the book toward the final stages, and for being such a wonderful source of support. Jan Cutler for her copyediting eye for detail. My agent, Diane Banks, who brought me to the dream publishing house, and for her continual guidance and encouragement.

I would also like to thank Mum and Dad for always cheering me on in whatever I do, Auntie Diane for her wonderful words of inspiration, Frankie Mullin and Nadine Brown for giving me an opportunity to spread the 'cosmic' word. And a very special thank you must go to John Wright who has been everything a soul mate should be and more, and without him, this book might still be just a dream.

Resources

Further Reading

If you would like to read into any of the subjects in the book in more detail, here is a short reading list of some of my favourite books to get you started:

Angel Inspiration: How to Change Your World with the Angels, Diana Cooper (Hodder Mobius, 2004)

A New Light on Angels, Diana Cooper (Findhorn Press, 2009)

The Crystal Healing Book, Judy Hall (Godsfield Press, 2005)

Aura Reading: How to Work with a Powerful Healing Energy, Cassandra Eason (Piatkus, 2000)

Chakra Clearing: Awakening Your Spiritual Power to Know and Heal, Doreen Virtue (Hay House, 2004)

Creative Visualization: Use the Power of Your Imagination to Create What You Want in Life, Shakti Gawain (New World Library, 2002)

Working with Meditation: Practical Ways of Healing and Transforming Your Life, Madonna Gauding (Godsfield Press, 2008)

Suppliers

I love spending time in Mysteries in Covent Garden as they have a great selection of books, crystals, incense, and all manner of holistic goodies. They have an online shop too so you can order from anywhere in the UK.

www.mysteries.co.uk

Crystals are in abundance at ISIS, they also have an online shop for all your shiny, sparkly needs. On a personal note, I chose my very first crystal from this store all those years ago.

www.thecrystalhealer.co.uk

Discussion

If you would like to get in touch and chat about any of the subjects discussed in the book, or to join in the forum discussions, you can contact me via my website:

www.stephaniebrookes.com

Index

Note: page numbers in **bold** refer
to diagrams.

affirmations 13–14, 104–6
air, clearing the 148–9
alpha waves 159
ambition 169
amethyst 164, 167, 171–2, 176, 178
angelic guides 23–4, 63–4
    see also Guardian Angels; spirit
        guides
angelic (sacred) space 67–8, 155–6
angelic/spirit world 72–3, 170
angelite 170, 173
angels 63, 65–6, 73, 140, 151
    see also archangels
animal guides 82–9
    see also pets
archangels 65–6, 74–8
arguments 144, 156
aroma 23, 150–1
attachment 6
auras 42–53, **43**, 61
    attractive 45–6
    and the chakras 54
    colour 23, 46–9
    and crystals 163, 169
    maintenance/cleansing 52–3
    sensing 23, 44–5, 49–52
automatic writing 101–4
azurite 167, 173

balance 5, 6, 8–9, 177
    see also material-spiritual equation/
        balance
baths, crystal 172
bears 86–7
'being in the moment' 161
bell ringing 149–50
beta waves 159
black 176, 177
bloodstone 169
blue 48, 56, 177, 180–1
blue lace agate 164, 168, 177
brain waves 159

calmness 177
cats 86, 143
chakras 54–61, **55**
    and the aura 54
    cleansing 60
    colour 55–8, 171, 179–82
    crown **55**, 56, 171–2, 180–1
    definition 59
    feeling 59–60
    healing with crystals 171, 172
    heart **55**, 56, 171, 180–1
    maintenance 58–60
    root **55**, 57–9, 171, 179–80, 182
    sacral **55**, 57, 171, 180, 182
    solar plexus **55**, 57–8, 171, 180–2
    spinning of 54
    third eye 31–3, **55**, 56, 167, 171, 180

throat **55**, 56, 171, 180–1
Chamuel, Archangel 77
change 6–7
channelling 102
    see also automatic writing
children
    and ghosts 138–9
    wishes/dreams of 91, 92
citrine 164, 168
clairaudience 24
claircognisance 24
clairgustance 24
clairsentience 23, 26
clairvoyance 23, 26
clapping 148–9, 153
cleaning
    crystals 172–3
    domestic/household 145–6
'clearing the air' 148–9
clothing 176–8, 181–2
clutter clearing 146
colour 3–4, 33, 34, 175–82
    of the aura 23, 46–9
    of the chakras 55–8, 171, 179–82
    of clothing 176–8, 181–2
    directory 46–9, 175, 176–8
    and your surroundings 178–9
communication 56, 74–5, 178
commuting 30
creativity 57, 76, 81
crown chakra **55**, 56, 171–2, 180–1
crystal balls, phoney 19–20
crystals 163–74, 176, 178
    and the aura 163, 169
    caring for 173–4
    choosing 174
    cleaning 172–3

energetic vibrations of 164, 165
getting the most out of 165–6
guide to 167–70
and meditation 164, 165–7
on the move 174
for pendulum dowsing 35
to heal chakras 171, 172
uses 164

dates, first 177
decorating 147
divination 37
dogs 86
dolphins 87
doubt 9–11
dowsing, pendulum 34–9, **35**
dream boards 108–10
dreams
    about soul mates 131
    and angelic communication 70
    and manifesting 96
    see also wishes/dreams

effort 96
emotions
    and the chakras 57
    'emotional baggage' 169
    energetic qualities of 44
energetic clearing *see* space clearing
energetic imprints 136–7
energy 41–61
    auras 42–53, **43**, 61, 163, 169
    boosts 41, 176
    chakras 31–3, 54–61, 171–2,
        179–82
    drains 41
    and manifesting 93
    see also negative energy

environments
  and colour 178–9
  see also homes
ESP (extrasensory perception) *see* sixth sense
exercises
  aura cleanse 53
  automatic writing 102–4
  bell ringing 150
  'bye-bye ghostie' 140–1
  chakra cleansing 60
  clapping 148–9
  cleansing with salt 152
  clearing clutter 146
  colourful meditations 179–81
  contacting Guardian Angels 68–9, 130
  crystal meditation 166–7
  dream boards 108–9
  face your fear 10–11
  feeling the aura 50–1
  feeling the chakras 59–60
  finding a soul mate 128–30
  grounding 28
  listening meditation 161–2
  manifesting 94–5, 97
  meeting your animal guide 84–5
  pendulum dowsing 36–8
  psychic protection 29–30
  seeing the aura 49–50
  sixth sense activation 32–3
  space clearing 146, 148, 150, 152–3
  viewing the aura 51–2
  wind downs 33–4
extrasensory perception (ESP) *see* sixth sense

fatigue 167
fear
  facing your 10–11, 115, 117, 170
  irrational 115
flowers 153
fortune-tellers, phoney 19–20
frankincense 151
friends 96, 168
  discussing spirituality with 15
  imaginary 139
  and manifesting 106–8
  negative 7
  psychic tasks to practice with 39
  special 6
future 19, 25, 39

Gabriel, Archangel 74–5, 81
ghosts x, 17
  cleansing exercises for 140–1
  definition 141
  poltergeists 141–2
  seeing 138–9
  signs of 138
  spiritual cleansing for 135–56
goddess, modern 3
goddess hour 157–83
  and colour 175–82
  and crystals 163–74
  and meditation 158–63
green 48, 56, 177, 180–1
grounding 27–8
guardian angels 5, 64–6, 78–9, 88
  building your connection with 69–71
  communication through dreams 96
  contacting 66–72, 73, 130, 151
  definition 67

names 69
questions to ask 70
seeing 23
signs of contact with 67, 70, 71–2
and soul mates 130, 131
'gut' feelings 13, 31, 57
see also intuition

Haniel, Archangel 76
happiness 13
hauntings
residual 136–7
see also ghosts
heart chakra **55**, 56, 171, 180–1
Higher Self 4–5, 11–16
and animal guides 87
and automatic writing 102–4
and the chakras 56
connection with 70, 76
definition 13
and intuition 97
and meditation 159
and pendulum dowsing 37
recognising messages from 12–16
as true friend 11–12
hippies ix, 2
homes, spiritual cleansing for 135–56

imaginary friends 139
imagination 29
see also visualisation
imbalance 8–9
impatience 132
incense 68, 140–1, 150–1, 153
indigo 56, 180
inner dialogue 161
inspiration 177

instinct 13
intention 92, 145, 173
interior design 154–6
intuition 13, 23–5, 31, 57, 97
and channelling 102
and colour choice 178
and crystal choice 174
and spirit guides 81–2
and your twin flame 118
see also 'gut' feelings

jade 169, 171
jasmine 151
jewellery 165
Jophiel, Archangel 76

karma 119–21

lapis lazuli 164, 168, 173
laptops 178
life lessons 115–17, 120–1
life paths, 'right' 100–1, 114
lifetimes (incarnations) 114
light
cleaning crystals with 173
and space clearing 154
white 29–31, 60, 140, 152
lions 87
Lotus position 160
love 56, 109
coming to an end 123
and crystals 170
scents for 151
and soul mates 113, 118, 126–32
see also relationships
Lower Self 4–5, 6–16
controlling your 9–11, 15–16

definition 8
and pendulum dowsing 36
spotting the work of 9, 14, 15
and your Higher Self 12, 13

make-up 3–4
malachite 169, 173
manifesting 91–111
    and affirmations 104–6
    and automatic writing 101–4
    and dream boards 108–10
    and friends 106–8
    guide to 93–7
    the 'right' path 100–1
    science of 93
    wish lists for 98–9
material life 4–6, 8, 57–9, 185
material-spiritual equation/balance
    4, 5, 8–9, 183
me time see goddess hour
meditation xi, 2, 158–63
    colourful 179–81
    and crystals 164, 165–7
    definition 158–9, 163
    listening 161–2
    positions for 160
    time for 162–3
    and your brain waves 159
mental movies 94, 97
Michael, Archangel 65–6, 75
moment, being in the 161
motivation 58
music 146, 153
mystery 176

nag champa 150
needs 57

negative energy
    in buildings 144
    protection from 30, 169
negative thinking 77, 99–100, 105
'New Age' movement 2

opportunity 7, 9–10
orange 48, 57, 177, 180, 182
orange calcite 164, 167, 173
orange carnelian 164, 169–70
owls 88

parking spaces 79
past lives 114–16
pendulum dowsing 34–9, **35**
peripheral vision 51–2, 67
personal time see goddess hour
pets
    healing for sick 75–6
    psychic 143
    watching over 81
    see also animal guides
photos/pictures 147, 179
pink 48, 56, 177, 180–1
plants 179
pleasures, simple 16
poltergeists 141–2
positive thinking 93, 97, 99–100, 105
precognition 25
protection 75
    see also psychic protection
psychic ability 19–40
    activating your sixth sense 31–3,
        176
    and everyday psychic events 20–1
    first steps 27–31
    getting in touch with your 26

as gift 21–2
natural 25–6
pendulum dowsing 34–9
practicing 21–2
precognition 25
prep work 27–31
and the senses 22
telepathy 25
wind downs 33–4
psychic attacks 30, 45
psychic imprints 136–7
psychic protection 29–31, 44–5
'psychic renaissance' 20
purple 47, 56, 176, 181

quartz
clear 167, 178
rose 164, 170, 171, 177
smoky 164, 170, 178
questions, asking 17

Raphael, Archangel 75–6
re-energising 176
record keeping 34, 71
red 47–8, 57, 176, 180, 182
red jasper 164, 169
reincarnation 114–16
relationships 77
coming to an end 123
first date impressions 177
soul mates 113, 118, 126–32
see also love
'right path', the 100–1, 114
root chakra 55, 57–9, 171, 179–80, 182
rose quartz 164, 170, 171, 177
'ruts', feeling stuck in 75

sacral chakra 55, 57, 171, 180, 182
sacred space 67–8, 155–6
salt, and space clearing 151–2
sandalwood 150
scents 23, 150–1
screensavers 178
self 185
feeling connected to 183
psychic 26
see also Higher Self; Lower Self
senses 22–4
psychic 23–4
sixth 22, 31–3, 56, 176
shopping 30
sixth sense 22, 31–3, 56, 176
smoky quartz 164, 170, 178
solar plexus chakra 55, 57–8, 171, 180–2
soul 113–14
soul groups 121–3
soul lessons 116–17
soul mates 113–33
confrontational 124–6
definition 117–19, 132
finding 126–32
romantic 113, 118, 126–32
twin flames 118–19
soul teachers 124–5
space, sacred 67–8, 155–6
space clearing 143–54
with aroma 150–1
with bell ringing 149–50
with clapping 148–9, 153
and cleaning 145–6
and decorating 147
definition 154
ending 152

with flowers 153
with intention 145
with light 154
with music 146, 153
with photos/pictures 147
purpose of 144–5
with salt 151–2
speedy 153
spirit guides 66, 78–82, 88, 139
  definition 82
  inability to see 73
  linking with 80–2
  privacy issues 82
  sensing 23–4
  working with 79–80
  see also angelic guides
'spiritual' ix–x, 14
spiritual life 5
spiritual-material equation/balance
    4, 5, 8–9, 183
spirituality ix–xi, 185
  common ground 6
  definition ix–x, 1–18
  history of 2
  'pick and mix' x, 3–4, 16–17
  starting out 17–18
  stereotypes of ix
stress overload 157
stress relief *see* goddess hour
subconscious mind 36
survival instinct 57
synchronicity 95–6

telepathy 25, 119
third eye 31–3, **55**, 56, 167, 171, 180
throat chakra **55**, 56, 171, 180–1
Tibetan tingsha bells 149

tigers 88
tiger's eye 164, 168, 171
twin flames 118–19

universe 129
  and life lessons 117
  and manifesting 93, 95–6, 100, 108
Uriel, Archangel 75

vibrations 72–3, 163–5
vision, peripheral 51–2, 67
visualisations 28–9
  chakra cleansing 60
  crystal meditation 166–7
  facing your fears 11
  finding a soul mate 128–9
  grounding 28
  manifesting 94–5
  meeting your animal guide 84–5
  psychic protection 29–30
  releasing negative thoughts 99–100
  sixth sense activation 31–3
  wind downs 33–4

wants 57
water, cleaning crystals with 173
white 49, 56, 177, 180–1
  light 29–31, 60, 140, 152
wish lists 98–9, 155
wishes/dreams, manifesting 91–111
wolves 88
writing, automatic 101–4

yellow 48, 57, 176, 180–2
yellow jasper 170

Zadkiel, Archangel 77